Language, Meaning and Style

ESSAYS IN MEMORY OF STEPHEN ULLMANN

STEPHEN ULLMANN

Language, Meaning and Style

ESSAYS IN MEMORY OF STEPHEN ULLMANN

Editorial Committee
T. E. Hope, †T. B. W. Reid, Roy Harris, and Glanville Price

LEEDS UNIVERSITY PRESS

Language, meaning and style.
1. Linguistics—Addresses, essays, lectures
2. Ullmann, Stephen—Addresses, essays, lectures
I. Hope, T.E.   II. Ullmann, Stephen
410   P125

ISBN 0-9507898-0-1

Printed in Great Britain by Leeds University Press

Editorial Note

The Editorial Committee record with regret the death on 30 August 1981 of one of their number, Emeritus Professor T. B. W. Reid. His encouragement, criticism, patience and editorial experience played a major part in bringing this commemorative volume to fruition.

Publication of the book has been made possible through financial support provided by the French Department of the University of Leeds, which is gratefully acknowledged. Our thanks are due to Mr G. O. Rees for his unremitting effort in reading and correcting proofs; and to Miss Julie Thornton for typing and secretarial services. The publication owes much to her expertise and initiative. The Editors also wish to express their gratitude to the Printing Service of the University of Leeds for understanding help freely given at every stage of production.

Contents

Stephen Ullmann, 1914–76

Stephen Ullmann's academic achievement is a classic example of the important contribution that twentieth-century European unrest has made to British scholarship. Born in Budapest immediately before the outbreak of the Great War, the son of a senior civil servant, he displayed a linguistic gift even from his schooldays which clearly indicated a future career in language studies. His obtaining a PhD of Budapest University *summa cum laude* at the age of twenty-two was none the less brilliant through being, in his case, predictable. A summary of the thesis was published in 1936: significantly, it brought together a Romance language and English, in a treatise analysing the influence of Italian on the Elizabethan literary usage. Though the major cultural language of his background was French his interests leaned strongly towards England and the British way of life. A month spent as guest in the home of a Cambridge don gave a receptive teenager the crucial impulse needed to transform a student's bent into a firm commitment which led him to take up permanent residence here in 1939 and to assume British nationality.

Two things set him squarely on his life's course: a shrewd appointment, and a momentous book. In 1946, thanks to the initiative of Professor Alan Boase and the late John Orr, Ullmann found himself in charge of the newly-created Department of Romance Philology and General Linguistics at Glasgow. Those who knew him then remember — as in a kind of golden age — the incomparable *soirées* at the Ullmanns' house in Prince's Terrace, presided over by Mrs Ullmann, as always, with elegance and distinction. To these gatherings came the greatest names in the linguistic world of the time on their way to renew contacts with Europe after a decade of exile.

The book was the one which must now stand as his masterpiece, the *Principles of Semantics* (1951). Despite the demands of war work in the monitoring service of the BBC Ullmann had found time to publish a dozen articles on topics as diverse as Sir Thomas More's dialogue on the Turco-Hungarian wars and the use of the past definite in modern French playwrights; he had also contrived to prepare material for a monograph on the newly-revived study of linguistic meaning, to which his attention had been drawn by the Budapest semanticist Professor Z. Gombocz. The *Principles* earned Ullmann his second doctorate, the DLitt; it also confirmed him as a scholar of international standing. There followed a series of books on related topics. *Words and their use*, a collection of essays, appeared in 1951. 1952 saw the publication of the work by which he came to be chiefly known in Europe, the *Précis de Sémantique Française*, written at the request of his friend Professor von Wartburg of Basle. *Semantics, an Introduction to the Science of Meaning* (1962), translated into six languages and reprinted on a number of occasions, is perhaps the work by which students and young researchers of many countries remember him best.

1952 was a year of change. It saw his appointment to the Chair of Romance Philology at Leeds, where he worked in harness with the late Professor G. T. Clapton — an epic combination of two unlike natures who were none the less as one in their scholarly integrity, greatness of heart and awesome physical presence. A less overt change took place in Ullmann's research interests. His first venture into the linguistic analysis of style dated back to articles published in 1945–46 on synaesthesia in the French Romantics. During the temporary respite from departmental administration which the Leeds Chair afforded he quickly achieved distinction in this new domain of stylistics (though 'semanticist' always remained the *epitheton constans* attached to his name, and even the last book, *Meaning and Style* (1973) still maintained the even balance between two disciplines which the title suggests). *The Image in the Modern French Novel* (1960) followed the more eclectic *Style in the French Novel* of 1957, and their success led him to launch the Language and Style series, of which he wrote the first volume under that title in 1964. It was at this time that he began to be surrounded by an entourage of postgraduate students who accompanied him for the rest of his life and began to populate French and Romance departments in the new universities and polytechnics, particularly after his move to Oxford in 1968. He was as indefatigable a correspondent as he was a reader, and this together with his research contacts made him one of the most informed academics of his day. To this formidable endowment was added a consummate skill in exposition. He revivified the despised generality of things, giving form and finiteness to that which was amorphous or problematical, and earning the gratitude even of those who felt that on occasions he cut corners a little. Constantly in demand as a speaker, he never refused to oblige, whether he was invited to address a local group of amateurs or to give the Twentyman lecture to the Modern Language Association. His academic duties farther afield included lecturing tours in France, Germany, Holland, Belgium, Portugal, Finland, Yugoslavia, Canada, the USA, and India, while he acted as external examiner to three East African universities. He held visiting Professorships at Toronto in 1964 and 1966, at Ann Arbor in 1965 and at Canberra in 1974. From 1970 to the year of his death Ullmann was a distinguished President of the Philological Society, a position which he greatly appreciated and to which he devoted unsparing energy.

Ullmann's translation to the Chair of the Romance Languages at Oxford, with the Professorial Fellowship at Trinity, was the summit of his career. Yet it enhanced rather than altered the pattern of activity he had already mapped out for himself. He could have opted to be the traditional bookish incumbent of an Oxford Chair; but like his predecessor T. B. W. Reid he chose to combine teaching and research with service to the Faculty and willingly took his share of committee chores inseparable from the life of a collegiate university. In doing so he won many firm friendships while acquiring no enemies. For Stephen Ullmann was first and foremost a man of peace. Criticism saddened him — and both his brand of semantics and of stylistics brought sharp criticism from some quarters — yet he forbore to reply in kind, steadfastly refusing to accept enmity from any colleague or to give way to it himself.

Though a staunch democrat inside and outside the university walls, Ullmann was no radical. In many ways he was an establishment figure of linguistics, holding uncompromisingly to the approaches which he knew to be traditionally sound. He had a great deal in common with the objective yet humanistic positivism of Bally and Meillet, or the neo-idealism of Leo Spitzer (another personal friend). Yet he was entirely *au fait* with modern trends; when he acted as chairman for a paper or at a symposium (as often happened) his gift for understanding the ideas and terminology of linguists of all schools in the minutest detail was quite extraordinary. His scholarship was so enterprising and varied that it is difficult and perhaps in any case too early to give each element its true weight. Encyclopaedic knowledge over many fields, single-mindedness in furthering his discipline, exceptional gifts as an inspirer and director of research, scruple and urbanity in personal relations — all these attributes spring to mind: and with them comes the realization that all were most particularly bound up with the physical presence of their animator, a presence denied to us from now on.

It is a sad irony that in the normal course of events Stephen Ullmann's colleagues would have been thinking today of preparing a *Festschrift* for his impending retirement. As it is, a commemoration volume must suffice to show how highly his friends and colleagues regarded him and what a profound debt they owed to his teaching.

This collection of essays is presented to Mrs Susie Ullmann and to Diana, Michael and Patricia as a tribute to the memory of a great scholar and a small measure of consolation for their loss.

T.E.H.

The Problem of Metaphor

JONATHAN CULLER

Professor of English and Comparative Literature, Cornell University

Rhetoric, which was once rumoured to have died in the nineteenth century, now appears to be a flourishing discipline, or at least a very active field. No year passes without new conferences on the nature of metaphor or special issues of scholarly journals devoted to the problem of metaphor.[1] Our illustrious forbears in the field of rhetoric, Quintilian, Puttenham, Dumarsais, and Fontanier, would doubtless have been delighted at this revival of interest in rhetoric, but they would have been puzzled, I believe, at the extraordinary privilege accorded to metaphor. Why metaphor? they might have asked. Why not organize a symposium on simile or synecdoche, on metalepsis or meiosis, or on such complex figures as anadiplosis, alloiosis or antapodosis? Metaphor is an important figure, they would have conceded, but by no means the only figure. Why should it usurp the attention of modern students of rhetoric?

Indeed, what seems to have happened is that as the scope and status of rhetoric has been reduced, that of metaphor has been amplified. In the days when rhetoric was, as Aristotle called it, a 'counterpart' of dialectic and logic, or when it encompassed, as in Cicero's account, invention, arrangement, style, memory, and delivery, then metaphor was simply one prominent stylistic device, one of the many categories defined by rhetorical theory. Today, however, it scarcely seems an exaggeration to say that metaphor is more important, more respectable, than rhetoric itself. We all

---

[1] Several recent examples, and there are doubtless others, are: Conference on Metaphor and Thought, University of Illinois, September 1977; Symposium on Metaphor, University of Chicago, February 1978; Interdisciplinary Conference on Metaphor, University of California at Davis, April 1978; Conference on Philosophy and Metaphor, University of Geneva, June 1978.

Two journal issues devoted to metaphor are *New Literary History*, 6, no 1 (1974) and *Critical Inquiry*, 5, no 1 (1978).

acknowledge the importance of metaphor and are therefore willing to grant, perhaps, a certain status to a discipline which studies metaphor. To put it crudely, it is only the fact that rhetoric studies metaphor that enables it to be more than 'insincere or grandiloquent language', which is certainly the primary contemporary meaning of *rhetoric*. It may well be that what is at stake in the privileging of metaphor is rhetoric itself.

I am suggesting, in short, that today metaphor is no longer one figure among others but the figure of figures, a figure for figurality; and I mean this not figuratively but quite literally: that the reason we can devote journals and conferences to metaphor is that metaphor is not just the literal name for a trope based on resemblance but is, on the contrary, a figure for figurality in general. Thus the term *metaphor* in discussions of 'the nature of metaphor' or 'the problem of metaphor' already poses some of the central questions that are at issue: how can one characterize the difference between the literal and the figurative here? What is the status of that difference? What happens when *metaphor* operates in this way? What is achieved by this figure?

We can begin to understand the situation with the help of a passage from Stephen Ullmann's *Language and Style*, which sets forth in exemplary fashion the argument that is doubtless covertly at work in many contemporary discussions of metaphor. In 'The Nature of Imagery', an essay which summarizes and refines the conclusions reached in his books *Style in the French Novel* and *The Image in the Modern French Novel*, Ullmann distinguishes two types of imagery: the metaphorical, which is based on a relationship of similarity, and the metonymical, which is based on an external relationship of contiguity. When the narrator of *Du Côté de chez Swann* speaks of 'la couleur vive, empourprée et charmante' of the name *Champi* (in George Sand's novel *François le Champi*), this may seem to be a striking metaphorical image,

> yet if we look more closely at the context we notice that the connection between the colour and the name is metonymic, not metaphorical; it is based, not on some hidden resemblance or analogy, but on a purely external relation: the accidental fact that the book had a red binding.[2]

Metonymies, he argues, will generally lack the 'originality and expressive power of metaphor' because instead of forging new links or uncovering new resemblances they are motivated by relationships of spatial juxtaposition; but occasionally, as in the example cited, they do give rise to

[2] Stephen Ullmann, *Language and Style* (Oxford: Blackwell, 1964), p 178.

what may be called a genuine metaphorical effect: in their expressive force
they achieve the metaphorical quality of 'an authentic image'. Metonymies
are interesting, in other words, only when they resemble metaphors; and
moreover, Ullmann continues, 'it should be added at once that the vast
majority of images are metaphorical; the remarks that follow will therefore
be confined to this type'.[3] While insisting in principle on the distinction
between the metaphorical and the metonymical, Ullmann argues that
interesting cases of the latter can be assimilated to the former so that a
discussion of imagery can be a discussion of metaphor alone.

This argument not only shows how the privileging of metaphor might
arise and be justified but also will help to indicate, if we pursue its
implications, what is at stake here. We began with a distinction between
two figures: metaphor, based on the perception of an essential similarity,
and metonymy, based on a merely accidental or contingent connection.
Now an analyst might for various reasons prefer to restrict his study of
imagery to figures of the first kind, but at this point he would have to admit
that the study of imagery ought to cover both cases. But if it is argued that
the interesting, expressive, or worthwhile examples of the figure based on
accident do in fact reveal or express essential properties and therefore
deserve to be assimilated to the figures based on essences, then it seems that
one is no longer confronted with two distinct classes of figures, both of
which should be encompassed by a study of imagery. On the contrary, one
could regard the existence of figures based on accident as something of an
accident, or at least not relevant to the essential functions and qualities of
figurative language. Setting aside the accidental and focusing on essentials,
we can discuss imagery under the heading of *metaphor*, a term which applies
literally to metaphors and figuratively to metonymies, or at least to those
metonymies which are worthy of our interest.

This setting aside of the accidental is important because of its bearing on
the cognitive status of rhetoric and thus ultimately on the value of rhetoric.
If rhetoric were assumed to encompass both metaphor and metonymy,
both essential resemblances and accidental connection, it might be difficult
to make compelling claims for the value of rhetorical devices. But if the
exemplary cases of metonymy can be brought under the heading of
metaphor and the other cases set aside as inessential, then the situation is

[3] *Ibid.*

B

very different. Of all the figures metaphor is the one that can most easily be defended or justified on cognitive grounds. 'The child is father to the man' presents the process of maturation in a new light; 'the foul rag and bone shop of the heart' implies a rather unusual account of human sensibility; 'the slings and arrows of outrageous fortune' presents an attitude towards fortune that one could accept or dispute. Whatever may be true of other figures, metaphors generally make claims that could in principle be restated as propositions, albeit with difficulty and prolixity. Doubtless for this reason, metaphor has long been thought of as the figure *par excellence* through which the writer can display creativity and authenticity: his metaphors are read as artistic inventions grounded in perceptions of relations in the world.

In privileging metaphor and making it the heading under which to discuss figurality in general one thus asserts the responsibility and authenticity of rhetoric; one grounds it in the perception of resemblances in experience, in intimations of essential qualities. One represses or sets aside rhetoric as a non-referential play of forms by taking as representative of rhetoric or figure in general a figure whose referentiality can be defended: in 'the sessions of sweet silent thought' the legal metaphor of 'sessions' tells us something about the act of rememoration, but admirers of the alliteration of 'sessions of sweet silent' might find it hard to claim that this formal device predicates something of the event. Small wonder, then, that defences of poetry have always appealed not to ends achieved by assonance, metonymy, hendiadys, etc, but to something very much like the function of metaphor: poetry presents human experience to us in a new way, giving us not scientific truth but a higher imaginative truth, the perception of fundamental connections and relationships. By taking metaphor as the representative figure one relegates to a problematical limbo the long list of figures with classical names that involve essentially formal processes of ordering, re-ordering, repetition; and one thereby makes it easier to defend literature as a mode of vision whose language is functional. No wonder modern interest in rhetoric is focused on metaphor, since the respectability, the value of rhetoric and of literature itself are involved.

But Ullmann's argument is interesting not only because it illustrates and helps to explain how contemporary focus on metaphor is justified; it also inaugurates an investigation of the relation between metaphor and metonymy which has very interesting results. Roman Jakobson in his 'Two

Aspects of Language and Two Types of Aphasic Disturbances' had argued that aphasia afflicts either the paradigmatic or the syntagmatic axis of language. 'The relation of similarity is suppressed in the former, the relation of contiguity in the latter type of aphasia.'[4] Even in normal linguistic activity, discourse will develop primarily through similarity or through contiguity. 'The metaphoric way would be the most appropriate term for the first case and the metonymic way for the second, since they find their most condensed expression in metaphor and metonymy respectively.' These two 'poles' of language are, Jakobson suggests, in a relationship of competition such that one or the other will prevail in a given discourse. Metaphor is the mode of poetry, particularly of romanticism and symbolism, whereas metonymy is the mode of realism.

Against Jakobson's claim that these two tropes represent the opposition between the most fundamental aspects of language, Ullmann noted in his discussion of Proust's imagery the potentially intimate relationship between them and the difficulty of separating the metaphorical from the metonymic in synesthetic imagery.[5] Citing this discussion ('C'est sans doute à Stephen Ullmann que revient le mérite d'avoir le premier . . . relevé la présence dans l'"imagerie" proustienne, à côté des fameuses métaphores, de transpositions typiquement métonymiques'),[6] Gérard Genette takes it a step further, arguing that many of Proust's most characteristic metaphors are generated by metonymy: if the steeples of Saint-André-des-Champs are described in terms appropriate to ears of corn and those of Saint-Mars-le-Vêtu as fish with mossy reddish scales, it is because the first rise out of the fields of grain while the second are by the sea.[7] The description functions metaphorically but is generated by a metonymic transfer, so that one can speak of metaphor supported by metonymy.

> Le glissement métonymique ne s'est pas seulement 'déguisé', mais bien transformé en prédication métaphorique. Ainsi, loin d'être antagonistes et incompatibles, métaphore et métonymie se soutiennent et s'interpénètrent, et faire sa part à la seconde ne consistera pas à en dresser une liste concurrente en face de celle des

---

[4] Roman Jakobson, *Fundamentals of Language* (The Hague: Mouton, 1956), p 76.
[5] Stephen Ullmann, *Style in the French Novel* (Cambridge University Press, 1957), pp 196–207.
[6] Gérard Genette, 'Métonymie chez Proust', *Figures III*, Collection Poéique (Paris: Seuil, 1972), pp 41–63; p 41.
[7] *Ibid*, pp 42–3.

métaphores, mais plutôt à montrer la présence et l'action des relations de 'coexistence' à l'intérieur même du rapport d'analogie: le rôle de la métonymie *dans la métaphore*.[8]

Gérard Genette also develops Ullmann's brief indication that involuntary memory in Proust is based on metonymy, so that the capture of essences which is said to result from this process of reliving the past in the present depends on a metonymic connection.[9] But at this point one might begin to wonder whether one is in fact dealing with a case of co-operation and harmonious coexistence of metaphor and metonymy, since the capture or perception of essences, if it is to mean anything or have any value, must be distinguished from the purely fortuitous or accidental relationships brought about by juxtaposition. Consider this famous passage from *Le Temps retrouvé* concerning metaphor, truth and essences, which Ullmann quotes:

> La vérité ne commencera qu'au moment où l'écrivain prendra deux objets différents, posera leur rapport analogue dans le monde de l'art à celui qu'est le rapport unique de la loi causale dans le monde de la science, et les enfermera dans les anneaux d'un beau style, ou même, ainsi que la vie, quand en rapprochant une qualité commune à deux sensations, il dégagera leur essence en les réunissant l'une et l'autre pour les soustraire aux contingences du temps, et les enchaînera par les liens indescriptibles d'une alliance de mots.[10]

In praising metaphor as revealing a truth which is the artistic analogue of a scientific law, Proust asserts a contrast between the metaphorical discovery of a-temporal essences and a different kind of connection, an accidental juxtaposition of items in time. So if it were to turn out that metonymies were at work in Proustian metaphors, this would not be so innocent or happy a co-operation as Genette implies. Indeed, the intermingling of metaphor and metonymies would have implications for the kinds of claims that could be made concerning metaphor. It is precisely this line of argument that Paul de Man has developed in a masterly analysis of a particularly salient passage in Proust, a passage which explicitly identifies the value of literature and of reading with the metaphorical perception of essences, but whose powerful and persuasive metaphors, de

---

[8] *Ibid*, p 42.
[9] *Ibid*, pp 55–8. Ullmann's remark is in *Style in the French Novel*, p 197.
[10] Quoted by Ullmann, *ibid*, p 191.

Man shows, turn out to depend upon a metonymy, an accidental connection of precisely the sort to which metaphor has been contrasted.

The passage from *Du Côté de chez Swann* describes Marcel reading in his room during the summer. His grandmother, of course, wants him to play rather than to sit reading, to be outside rather than inside, and Marcel goes on to defend reading as giving him more dramatic adventures and more direct access to people and passions than he would have gained by playing outside. This familiar if unusually explicit reflection on the value of reading is introduced and given a foundation by the passage which claims that Marcel's withdrawal from the light, heat, and activity of summer to the cool tranquillity of his room is not in fact a sacrifice, nor does it involve any cognitive loss. On the contrary, it is claimed, by withdrawing to his room he is able to grasp the essence of summer in a way that he could not if he were outside playing. 'L'obscure fraîcheur de ma chambre,' the narrator claims, 'offrait à mon imagination le spectacle total de l'été, dont mes sens, si j'avais été en promenade, n'auraient pu jouir que par morceaux.'[11] And in explaining how it is that the essence of summer can be transferred or transported to him as he sits inside, he insists on the distinction between a transfer of meaning based upon the accidental contiguity of sensations, which would be a metonymical transfer of associations, and a transfer of meaning based on necessary connections, a metaphorical revelation of essence. The 'sensation de la splendeur et de la lumière' is conveyed to him

> par les mouches qui exécutaient devant moi, dans leur petit concert, comme la musique de chambre de l'été: elle ne l'évoque pas à la façon d'un air de musique humaine, qui, entendu *par hasard* à la belle saison, vous la rappelle ensuite; elle est unie à l'été par un *lien plus nécessaire*: née des beaux jours, ne renaissant qu'avec eux, contenant un peu de *leur essence*, elle n'en réveille pas seulement l'image dans notre mémoire, elle en certifie le retour, la *présence effective*, ambiante, immédiatement accessible.[12] (my italics)

But in order to persuade that nothing essential of summer is lost in this transfer and that Marcel reading indoors does indeed experience 'le spectacle total de l'été', the passage must manoeuvre in such a way that the notion of heated activity, which is associated with the scene outside, be transferred to the inside. This transfer is brought about in

[11] Marcel Proust, *A la recherche du temps perdu* (Paris: Gallimard, 1954), I, p 83.
[12] *Ibid.*

the paragraph immediately following which begins with the claim previously quoted that 'l'obscure fraîcheur de ma chambre . . . offrait à mon
imagination le spectacle total de l'été', and which continues with the
assertion that this

> obscure fraîcheur . . . s'accordait bien à mon repos qui (grâce aux
> aventures racontées par mes livres et qui venaient de l'émouvoir)
> supportait, pareil au repos d'une main immobile au milieu d'une eau
> courante, le choc et l'animation d'un torrent d'activité.

In the context of a description of summer the image of a hand
feeling the cool sensation of the running brook is seductive, but this image
also works, as de Man says, to reconcile

> l'immobilité fraîche de la main avec la chaleur de l'action. Ce
> transfert est effectué, toujours dans la même phrase, lorsqu'il est
> dit du repos qu'il supporte 'un torrent d'activité'. L'expression
> 'torrent d'activité' n'est pas, ou plus, une métaphore mais un
> cliché, une métaphore morte ou endormie qui a perdu sa valeur
> suggestive pour ne plus avoir qu'un sens propre. 'Torrent d'acti-
> vité' signifie simplement 'beaucoup d'activité', une quantité
> d'activité susceptible d'agiter quelqu'un au point de l'échauffer. La
> chaleur s'introduit ainsi subrepticement dans le texte, bouclant
> les polarités opposées en une chaîne continue et permettant
> l'échange des propriétés antithétiques: du moment où le repos
> peut être actif et chaud sans pourtant perdre sa qualité de repos,
> l'action d'abord fragmentée de la réalité peut devenir totale sans pour
> autant perdre sa qualité de réalité.[13]

But this image which is essential to the overall success of the
passage is, as de Man argues, metonymical rather than metaphorical: it
is based first of all on the accidental association or linkage of the words
torrent and *activité* in a cliché or idiomatic expression (accidental since the
essential and literal features of 'torrent' are not important to the idiom); and
secondly on the fact that the juxtaposition of the cliché *torrent d'activité*
with the image of the hand in the water reawakens, as an effect of
contiguity, the association of *torrent* with water. The power and persuasive-
ness of this text, which celebrates reading and sequestration as a mode of

---

[13] Paul de Man, 'Proust et l'allégorie de la lecture', in *Mouvements premiers: Etudes critiques
offertes à Georges Poulet* (Paris: Corti, 1973), p 238. A much briefer discussion of this passage
appears in de Man's 'Semiology and Rhetoric', *Diacritics*, 3, no 3 (Fall, 1973). Both articles
are included in his *Allegories of Reading* (New Haven — London: Yale UP, 1979).

capturing essences after the fashion of metaphorical language, turns out to depend on metonymical effects of contiguity. 'Cette structure', de Man concludes,

> est complexe mais caractéristique du langage proustien. Dans un passage qui contient des métaphores réussies, c'est-à-dire séduisantes et 'vraies', et qui par ailleurs affirment explicitement la supériorité poétique et epistémologique de la métaphore sur la métonymie, la conviction est emportée par un jeu de figures dans lequel une structure métonymique se déguise en métaphore.[14]

If with this analysis in mind one turns back to the cases which Genette and Ullmann cite, one sees that in these and other situations a metaphorical description of essences, offered and celebrated as an example of the kind of revelation of essences and imaginative truth which literary language can achieve, depends on accidental associations, metonymical contiguity, and indeed that the metonymical associations help to render more plausible the metaphorical characterizations (as in the case of the steeples mentioned above) which are claimed to be essential rather than contingent. The privileging of metaphor over metonymy is an assertion of the cognitive value and respectability of literary language (relegating the accidental play of verbal associations and chance juxtapositions to an ancillary status where it can be ignored), but this privileging is made possible only by the incorporation within the orbit of metaphor of certain metonymical effects.

We can see further that this complex privileging of metaphor which was described in Ullmann's discussion is not simply a move made by critics and theorists who might naturally be inclined to concentrate on tropes that are cognitively defensible.[15] It is also a move made in literary works themselves which characteristically suggest that their descriptions are generated not by chance associations but by the perception of fundamental similarities. There are thus powerful forces at work to make 'metaphor' both the opposite of metonymy and other tropes based on accident and the authoritative representative of figurative language in general: the figure for figurality.

---

[14] De Man, 'Proust et l'allégorie de la lecture', p 239.

[15] Jakobson argues that since the relationship between the critic's metalanguage and the text he is discussing is metaphorical, he 'possesses a more homogeneous means to handle metaphor, whereas metonymy, based on a different principle, easily defies interpretation'. *Fundamentals of Language*, p 81.

An understanding of the problem of metaphor certainly would require an appreciation of the complex relationship I have been trying to outline between metaphor and other verbal figures, but of course the notion of metaphor as an instance of figurative language depends upon the opposition between the literal and the figurative which is at least as complex and elusive as the opposition between the metaphorical and the metonymic. There seem to be two ways of thinking about this problem, which we might christen the *via philosophica* and the *via rhetorica*. The first locates metaphor in the gap between sense and reference, in the process of thinking of an object, event, etc, *as* something: thinking of the heart as a foul rag and bone shop or of fortune as an enemy wielding slings and arrows. This is the approach one takes when one wishes to emphasize the cognitive respectability of metaphor, because one can argue that cognition itself is essentially a process of seeing something as something and thus make metaphor an instance of general cognitive processes at their most creative or speculative.

However, precisely because this approach assimilates metaphor to general cognitive processes, it makes it difficult to establish any firm distinction between the literal and the metaphorical. Since to use language at all is to treat something as a member of a class, see it as an instance of some category, language itself seems to be metaphorical. A non-metaphorical language would consist of logically proper names only; but, as it turns out, logically proper names are something natural languages do not have.[16] To call something by a name in a natural language is to ascribe to it some properties, to bring it under some loose heading. It would seem, then, that as soon as we speak we engage in metaphor.

If we pursue this line of argument we reach the paradoxical conclusion that is outlined, for example, by Rousseau in his *Essai sur l'origine des langues* or by Vico in the *Scienza Nuova*, that language originates in metaphor and that figurative language precedes literal language. Though this argument may be coupled with claims about primitive modes of perception — that the first men were poets — it need not be, since the act of grouping distinct particulars under a common heading on the basis of perceived or imagined resemblance, which is the central act in any narrative of the origin of language, corresponds to the classical definition of metaphor: substitution

---

[16] F. E. Sparshott mentions this in his elegant and interesting discussion, '"As" or The Limits of Metaphor', *New Literary History*, 6, no 1 (Autumn 1974), p 79.

on the basis of resemblance.[17] If language originates in figure and is essentially metaphorical, then what we call literal meaning or literal language is nothing but figurative language whose figurality has been forgotten.

The appropriateness of this claim may seem questionable when one focuses on what one thinks of as ordinary terms, such as *chair, book, tree, sleep*; but it is easy to grasp when one considers an appellation where we still have some notion of the act of cognition involved: for example, study of the behaviour of bees and the identification of certain resemblances between their communicative behaviour and human communication led some writers to extend the term *language* to 'the language of bees'. It may well be that now this expression is no longer regarded as figurative but literal, in which case it would be an example of literal language as figurative language whose figurality has been forgotten.

The most famous statement of this position, of course, is Nietzsche's in the essay 'Über Wahrheit und Lüge im aussermoralischen Sinn':

> What is truth? A moving army of metaphors, metonymies and anthropomorphisms, in short a *summa* of human relationships that are being poetically and rhetorically sublimated, transposed, and beautified until, after long and repeated use, a people considers them as solid, canonical, and unavoidable. Truths are illusions whose illusionary nature has been forgotten, metaphors that have been used up and have lost their imprint and that now operate as mere metal, no longer as coins.[18]

I have noted above that the *via philosophica* gives metaphor considerable cognitive respectability, but as this passage from Nietzsche makes clear, that respectability is achieved at some cost. If metaphor is identified with truth itself, that may seem to elevate metaphor, but it undermines truth. The line of argument that gives metaphor cognitive respectability ends by abolishing cognitive respectability. In general one might observe that any attempt to ground trope or figure in truth always contains the possibility of reducing truth to trope.

If the *via philosophica* leads to a problematizing of the distinction between literal and figurative which it has set out to explore and if it concludes with a paradoxical assertion of the priority of the figurative over the literal, it might seem wise to try the other road. The *via rhetorica* locates metaphor not in the gap

---

[17] For discussion see de Man, 'Theory of Metaphor in Rousseau's *Second Discourse*', in *Romanticism*, ed D. Thorburn and G. Hartman (Ithaca — London: Cornell University Press, 1973).

[18] Friedrich Nietzsche, *Werke*, ed Karl Schlechta (Munich: Hanser, 1956), 3, p 311.

between sense and reference but in the space between what is meant and what is said: between a literal or proper verbal expression and a periphrastic substitute. By thus placing itself on the terrain of language itself, it avoids the consideration of cognition which led the *via philosophica* to find all language fundamentally figurative. Indeed, by assuming that metaphorical language is another way of saying something which could in principle be said literally, the *via rhetorica* makes the potential virtues of metaphor not cognitive but stylistic: a metaphor may be more concise and vivid than the corresponding literal version.

This approach works quite well for expressions such as *John is a fox*, where we can identify *fox* as the metaphorical substitute for a literal formulation such as *devious, crafty creature*. Indeed, it is under this heading that one should locate traditional definitions of metaphor as a substitution based on resemblance, whether resemblance be defined in terms of common semantic features, membership in a common class, or proportional analogy (Aristotle's A:B::C:D). The difficulties arise in situations where we want to claim that a sequence is metaphorical without our being able to compare the figurative detour or substitute with the literal expression which it replaces. Literary critics are often inclined to insist that creative and successful metaphors say something that cannot be said any other way and must not be regarded as simply vivid substitutes for a literal statement. The value of 'foul rag and bone shop of the heart', they might argue, lies in the fact that its full import cannot be approximated by any paraphrase.

The rhetorician may be inclined to regard this attitude as a kind of mystical defensiveness which should not be allowed to obstruct theory. After all, he would argue, if we claim to understand a metaphor then in principle we ought to be able to say what we understand by it, and it is precisely the contrast between the expression itself and what we understand by it that is the difference between the literal and the metaphorical. It may be difficult to produce a literal statement in some cases, but in principle these cases are no different from *John is a fox*. Certainly the rhetorician would wish to insist that the existence of difficult cases is no grounds for refusing to take simple cases as the norm.

But there is a certain perversity in an account of metaphor which works well for highly uninteresting and even artificial figures of replacement and which breaks down, or at least becomes relatively useless, in the case of the creative, suggestive literary metaphors which interest us most. Indeed, the problems of this approach are nicely summed up by the case of what rhetoricians have called catachresis. Catachresis occurs, according to Fontanier, when a sign already assigned to a first idea is assigned to a new idea which had no expression — that is to say, where there is no existing literal expression which the figurative designation is replacing.[19] One example of catachresis would be *head of lettuce*, in which *head*, which is already assigned one idea, is assigned to another idea which has no other designation. Another example of catachresis, however, would be a truly creative metaphor which names something that previously had no name, a metaphor which discloses or identifies something that we have no other way to describe. In both cases there is no substitution of a figurative expression for a literal one — which puts in question the claim that it is the contrast between the literal and the figurative which constitutes metaphors. And we cannot adopt the expedient of excluding catachresis from the domain of metaphors (on the grounds that so-called 'dead' metaphors are no longer metaphors), because truly creative metaphors also lack this crucial contrast between the literal paraphrase and the figurative denomination.

Thus, the *via rhetorica* also seems to lead us to a point where the distinction between the literal and the metaphorical becomes problematical. We started with a normal, literal use of language against which was to be set the deviant figurative use and sought to define the second precisely by its contrast with the first; but we then came upon cases where the first was not something given but at best something to be constructed with difficulty. In both approaches to metaphor, then, it proves difficult to maintain the priority of the literal over the figurative, but since the figurative is defined as a deviation from the literal, on which it is thus said to depend, this reversal of priority creates problems for the distinction itself. In both cases the distinction between the literal and the metaphorical is essential yet thoroughly problematic.

The problem of metaphor, as it has been discussed here, involves two separate problems, two oppositions which are necessary to any account of metaphor but which prove awkward and paradoxical. The distinction between meta-

---

[19] Pierre Fontanier, *Les Figures du discours* (1821, reprinted Paris: Flammarion, 1977), pp 213–14.

phor and metonymy and that between the literal and the figurative turn out
to behave in surprisingly similar ways. In both cases we have a binary
opposition which is asymmetrical: one of the terms is treated as privileged,
as more fundamental, and in both cases the privileged term, seen as
cognitively respectable, is set against a certain rhetoricity, a linguistic
detour which is primarily ornamental. Metonymy, as opposed to metaphor, and the metaphorical, as opposed to the literal, are relegated to a
secondary status for reasons that are not at all difficult to grasp since they
seem fundamental to our culture's way of thinking about language.

In both cases, however, the asymmetry turns out to be unstable, and as
one explores further the logic of the situation, one discovers that the term
treated as secondary and derivative can be seen as basic. In the case of
metaphor and metonymy, not only does the power of certain metaphorical
passages or celebrations of metaphor depend upon metonymies, but we can
see that the privileging of the category itself can only be accomplished by
assimilating interesting metonymies to it. In the case of the literal versus the
figurative, the terms in which the figurative is defined so as to be
distinguished from the literal lead one, paradoxically, to recognize the
primacy of the figurative, either by identifying it with general cognitive
processes and seeing the literal as figures whose figurality has been
forgotten (this was the *via philosophica*) or by focusing on cases of
catachresis where the figure seems to work without being contrasted with
the literal (the *via rhetorica*).

Ideally, an article which describes the problems that make metaphor a
problem would conclude by offering an elegant and convincing solution.
But it may well be that there is no solution, that metaphor is not something
we could see clearly if only we could resolve these problems. It may be,
rather, that the domain of metaphor is constituted by these problems: the
unstable distinction between the literal and the figurative and the crucial yet
unmasterable distinction between essential and accidental resemblances.
What one can do by way of conclusion, however, is to shift ground
somewhat so as to see the problem in a different perspective.

The philosopher Donald Davidson claims, in an argument which is
definitely attractive, that discussions of the meaning of metaphorical
expressions are fundamentally in error. His argument can be succinctly
illustrated. Consider the simile, 'a geometrical proof is like a mousetrap'.
This sentence tells us that there is a similarity or similarities between a

geometrical proof and a mousetrap and doubtless enjoins us to think of possible similarities, but it does not tell us which features of the objects we should think of. There is no reason to claim that any particular similarities are part of the meaning of the sentence; the sentence simply asserts that there is a similarity. In the case of a metaphor, 'a geometrical proof is a mousetrap', theorists usually insist that to give the meaning of the metaphor is to identify the similarities in question, to define what is being predicated of geometrical proofs. But would it not be better to say that in asserting an identity the metaphor leads us to think about possible similarities but does not itself define them, and that no particular similarities are part of the meaning of the metaphor, any more than they are part of the meaning of the simile?[20] After all, if I say 'geometrical proofs are horrible', my assertion may lead people to think of properties which might provoke distaste, but to give the meaning of this sentence one does not need to produce a list of such properties.

Davidson's theory is attractive because of its simplicity, but such simplicity is usually purchased at the cost of complexity elsewhere, and that is certainly the case here. By denying that metaphors have any special meaning he makes necessary an elaborate account of the *effect* of metaphorical assertions, a complex analysis of responses to these false assertions of identity. Generally analysts of metaphor have assumed that metaphors communicate because they have a complex structure which must be described. They treat metaphors as tropes or devices, elements of a system, structures of *la langue* in its broadest sense, which have effects because of certain structural features. Davidson's theory claims that from the point of view of *la langue* and of system generally what we call metaphor is nothing more than a false assertion of identity and that the question of what is communicated by metaphor is a question about *parole*, language use, persuasion. It is not a matter of structure but of effect, and the study of metaphor should be a study of response.

This might well be a very fruitful line of enquiry. It would involve treating the notion of metaphor as a description of certain kinds of interpretive operations performed by readers when confronted with an incongruity in a text. In *Hamlet* when we encounter the sentence 'Look, the morn in russet mantle clad Walks o'er the dew of yon high eastern hill', we

---

[20] Donald Davidson, 'What Metaphors Mean', *Critical Inquiry*, 5, no 1 (Autumn 1978), p 39.

have various interpretive possibilities. We could assume that in the world of this play (which does, after all, contain ghosts) morn is a figure that walks over hills; we could posit that Horatio is hallucinating (the ghost has been too much for him); or we could assume that the morning here behaves in accordance with our usual models of verisimilitude and that the false assertion that morning 'walks' should lead us to reflect on the qualities of dawn. Extracting what might 'really' belong to dawn, we label the phrases 'metaphor' and read the constructed detour as an index of wonder and poetic intensity.

From this perspective of reading, metaphor is the name of one sort of move in an ongoing process of interpretation, but it would be a mistake to suppose that by adopting this perspective we avoid the problems that arose when we treated metaphor as a device or structure. Since we do not believe that responses to metaphorical expressions are random or purely personal phenomena, any analysis of response will attempt to account for responses by positing norms, conventions, in a word, structures. We shall need to distinguish a metaphorical interpretive move from a metonymical move; we shall also confront the problem of catachresis, albeit in another form.

Nevertheless this approach to metaphor as an example of language use rather than language structure, as an instance of *parole* rather than a structure of *la langue*, is promising, and one cannot predict precisely what insights it might yield. Stephen Ullmann once argued that stylistics should be regarded as a discipline parallel to linguistics with the same divisions as linguistics. One would therefore expect a distinction between *langue* and *parole* within the study of style and rhetoric. In stylistics as in linguistics, *la langue* is the privileged object of study, but there is always the alternative of attempting to describe phenomena from the perspective of language use rather than language structure. 'Each of the two approaches', Ullmann argued with the judicious even-handedness that characterized all his work, 'has its distinctive procedures which may be combined but must not be confused.'[21] This warning seems thoroughly apposite to the problem of metaphor.

---

[21] Ullmann, *Style in the French Novel*, p 5.

Truth-Conditional Semantics and Natural Languages

ROY HARRIS

Professor of General Linguistics in the University of Oxford

Using a language effectively for purposes of communication is generally taken to involve knowledge of what are conventionally called the 'meanings' of its words and word combinations. But what exactly these 'meanings' are, and what it is to know them, is far from clear. Diverse attempts to provide theoretical explications for such basic concepts constitute in large part the history of modern semantics. The particular approach to be discussed in what follows is one which proposes that the best way to explain the concept of the meaning of a sentence is by defining it in terms of a prior concept of 'truth'. As far as linguists are concerned, the test by which this or any other type of explication must be judged is whether it provides useful answers to the questions which must be asked in the course of any practical enterprise of constructing a semantic description of a natural language; eg whether an expression has one or more meanings, whether or not it differs in meaning from another expression, how it differs in meaning from other expressions, whether its meaning varies according to context, and so on. For if a theory has nothing, or nothing helpful, to say on such matters, then whatever other value it may have, it is of little relevance to linguistics.

The various current versions of truth-conditional semantics as applied to natural languages differ from one another in ways which do not affect the argument advanced in the present paper. By 'truth-conditional semantics' will be understood any theory which offers the following as its central tenet: that 'to know the meaning of a sentence is to know under what conditions one who utters it says something true'.[1]

The plausibility of such a theory appears to rest on two sorts of consideration. Negatively, truth-conditional theorists sometimes claim that, whatever the difficulties with truth-conditional semantics may be, at least it has certain advantages over other kinds of semantic theory. For example, Evans and McDowell[2] contrast truth-conditional semantics favourably with 'translational semantics', a term they use for any theory which assumes that 'the most that can be expected of a semantic theory is the setting up of translation rules'.[3] A translational semantic theory of a natural language gives translations of the expressions of the language into expressions of a chosen metalanguage.[4] Evans and McDowell point out that if no restriction at all were placed on the choice of a metalanguage, there would be nothing to prevent using the language under description as the metalanguage also, in such a way as to produce quite vacuous results. Clearly, however correct it may be to give 'elephant' as a gloss for the word *elephant*, any lexicographer who proceeded on that principle and so produced a dictionary consisting of nothing but matching columns of identical entries would have produced a work of no practical use whatsoever. However, various conditions may be imposed which obviate vacuous 'semantic descriptions' of this kind, and these conditions can be stated in terms of the correspondence between sentences of the object language and sentences of the metalanguage. One condition is that any meaningful and unambiguous sentence of the object language have just one sentence to translate it in the metalanguage. A second is that any ambiguous sentence of the object language have as many different translations in the metalanguage as it has ambiguities. A third is that a meaningless sentence of the object

---

[1] P. F. Strawson, *Meaning and Truth* (Oxford: Clarendon Press, 1970), p 24. Only declarative sentences will be considered here. The problems posed by non-declarative sentences, and by non-assertoric uses of declarative sentences, are not mentioned, since the usual method of dealing with such problems advocated by truth condition theorists consists in an attempt to show that these cases are amenable to treatment on the same lines as the declarative sentences (used assertorically in the 'normal' way). But this manoeuvre automatically fails if the treatment of declarative sentences is itself shown to be inadequate.

[2] G. Evans and J. McDowell (eds), *Truth and Meaning* (Oxford: Clarendon Press, 1976).

[3] *Op cit*, p viii.

[4] Castigated as 'translational semantics' is early transformational semantics as represented by Katz, Fodor and Postal, and one variety of generative semantics as represented by McCawley; but the criticism is not restricted to the work of transformationalists.

language have no translation in the metalanguage. A fourth is that if there is an entailment relation between two sentences of the object language there is a corresponding relation between the translation sentences in the metalanguage. Satisfaction of the first three of the foregoing conditions requires a metalanguage of which the sentences are free from syntactic or lexical ambiguity, and of the fourth that at least some simple lexical items in the object language be given complex translations in the metalanguage; for otherwise there will be no way of capturing the semantic relation between sentences such as *John is a bachelor* and *John is unmarried*. But conditions of this kind imposed on the metalanguage, Evans and McDowell argue, still allow the possibility that someone might have a grasp of the translational correspondences 'and yet not know what a single sentence of the language meant'. In order to understand that, he would need also to know what the sentences of the metalanguage meant, and 'this is knowledge of precisely the kind that was to be accounted for in the first place'.[5]

The acceptance of translational semantics, according to Evans and McDowell, is due to a mistaken acceptance of the impossibility of getting 'outside the circle of language'. But there is a way out, shown by Tarski: for 'the sentence "Snow is white" is true if and only if snow is white does not report a relation which the sentence "Snow is white" has to itself, but states at any rate *one* semantic property of the sentence by using it, in an exemplification of the very use which we might put it to in expressing our belief that snow is white'. Hence a semantic description along these lines, ie one which 'uses expressions to state meanings' instead of merely quoting translation equivalents will be 'immune to the objection which devastates translational semantics, namely that someone could know it without understanding the language of which it is a theory'.[6]

Similar attacks on translational semantics have been made by other philosophers and accepted by linguists. Kempson, for example, rejects the defence offered by Bierwisch that semantic features as employed in the metalanguage of semantic descriptions are symbols 'for the internal mechanisms by means of which such phenomena are perceived and conceptualised'[7] on the ground that if this is so 'the status of any semantic

---

[5] Evans and McDowell, *op cit*, p ix.

[6] *Ibid*, p x.

[7] M. Bierwisch, 'Semantics', in J. Lyons (ed), *New Horizons in Linguistics* (London: Penguin Books, 1970), p 181.

component(s) is in principle untestable since there is no means of testing a so-called perceptual construct'.[8] (This happens to be a particularly flagrant case of pot calling the kettle black, since although there may be no means of testing 'a so-called perceptual construct', there is no means of testing for truth in all conceivable cases either, which is what Kempson's preferred type of theory would require.)

The main point which needs to be made in the present context is that both the alleged objection to translational semantics and the supposed advantage of truth-conditional semantics are alike based upon misconceptions. What is valuable about the case presented by Evans and McDowell is that it spells out the misconceptions in such a lucid manner. The first misconception is that we can make sense of the notion of a 'meaning equivalence' relation of the kind required for translation without knowing anything at all about the communicational values of the items which stand as the terms linked by such a relation. In other words, there is no such concept as synonymy (either intralingual or interlingual) divorced from the communicational use of linguistic expressions. Thus while someone acquainted with just two languages (say French and English) might grasp the general import of a statement to the effect that eg French *bivalence* can be translated by English *bivalence*, even though he does not know how either word is used, this is only in virtue of his having already grasped what is involved in translation pairings like *chien* and *dog, aller* and *go*, and many others. Furthermore, unless he had a prior assurance that the two languages were isomorphic, he could never be sure whether the pairing stated for the unfamiliar items *bivalence* and *bivalence* is intended to be of exactly the same sort as for any other two expressions. What he could certainly never do would be to understand what a translational pairing of any French and English expressions involved, if he did not independently understand the communicational value of any expression in either language. And that is just the situation that has to be envisaged to validate the objection to translational semantics that a person might grasp the whole complex of translation equivalences 'and yet not know what a single sentence of the language meant'.

The concomitant misconception is that a system of Tarski-type formulations commits us to something more concrete than a system of translation equivalences. This may seem plausible so long as we confine our attention to

[8] R. M. Kempson, *Presupposition and the delimitation of semantics* (Cambridge: Cambridge UP, 1975), p 30.

single instances. Even so, it is question-begging to claim, as Evans and McDowell do, that to say 'that Pierre knows that something satisfies *"chauve"* if and only if it is bald is not to credit Pierre with knowledge of some relation between *"chauve"* and the English word "bald" — knowledge which he could have without knowing what either meant'.[9] For if Pierre did not know what either word meant, he could not know — in the relevant sense of 'know' — the relation between them (even though he might 'know' it in some irrelevant sense, eg through having been assured that such a relation obtained). To describe the totality of Pierre's linguistic knowledge in this way gets us no further, in the final analysis, than claiming that eg Pierre knows that something satisfies *'chauve'* if and only if it fulfils the same conditions as required for satisfaction of *'bald'*. Here, although we do not credit Pierre with knowledge of a translation equivalence, we state what he does know in terms which assume that translation equivalence. But the real question at issue is always the validity of the translation equivalence, not whether or not we are crediting Pierre with bilingual skills he does not possess.

A more positive case for truth-conditional semantics must stand or fall by the success with which it can in principle bridge the explanatory gap apparent on considering that knowing what a sentence means is, *prima facie*, something very different from knowing whether what someone says in using the sentence is true. Here the plausibility of truth-conditional semantics rests basically upon acceptance of what may be called the 'truth-determinacy' principle: ie that when a speaker uses a declarative sentence assertorically what he says has a determinate truth value.

The truth-determinacy principle appears, in a very large range of cases, at least not to conflict with the assumptions we make in appraising what people say in everyday conversation. For example, if someone says that it is raining in Birmingham (specifically, if he uses the English declarative sentence *It is raining in Birmingham* to make an assertion) we assume that what he says is either true or false, ie that either it is raining in Birmingham, as he says (in which case his assertion has the truth value 'true'), or it is not raining in Birmingham (in which case his assertion has the truth value 'false'

[9] Evans and McDowell, *ibid.*

or 'not true'). We assume, in other words, that what he says is relevant to a certain state of affairs in the world, and this state of affairs is what determines the truth or otherwise of his assertion. The notion that it was indeterminate whether or not it was raining in Birmingham would be one which flouted our basic conception of what it was to make such an assertion, and hence what it was to use a sentence like *It is raining in Birmingham* for purposes of communication.

In connexion with this claim it should be noted: (i) that it is no objection to point out that conceivably, on some occasions, meteorological conditions in Birmingham are such that all fluent speakers of English would be in doubt, or hopelessly divided, as to whether or not it was raining. On the contrary, this supports the validity of the truth-determinacy principle. For if that principle were not accepted, there would be nothing to be in doubt or divided about; (ii) that whether or not the truth of *p* is determinate is not, in any case, to be confused with whether there is doubt or uncertainty as to the truth of *p*, which is a psychological question; (iii) that although it may suit the purposes of logicians to devise many-valued systems of logic, everyday usage in natural languages quite clearly relies on a simple two-valued system. Thus whereas to admit 'I cannot tell whether it is raining in Birmingham or not', or 'No one can tell for sure whether it is raining in Birmingham or not', makes perfectly good sense, to say 'I was in Birmingham and it was neither raining nor not raining' does not unless treated as a loose paraphrase of, eg, 'I was in Birmingham and I could not decide whether it was raining or not'.

If all declarative sentences were like *It is raining in Birmingham* in the relevant respects, then all assertions would be claims to the effect that at a certain time (t_1) the world was in a certain state (W_1), eg that it was then in a state such that certain meteorological conditions obtained in Birmingham. In order to specify W_1 fully, it would be necessary to specify many more facts about the state of the world at t_1. But that such facts could in principle be specified also appears to be an assumption intrinsic to our use of sentences like *It is raining in Birmingham*. Thus someone who asserts that it is raining in Birmingham will also, in the normal course of events, suppose that it is also at the same time either raining or not raining elsewhere, eg in Manchester, Coventry, Edinburgh, etc (although whether it is or not need not concern him). Furthermore, he will suppose that, at the time in question, the population of Birmingham is of a certain size, either greater than or not greater than the population of eg Manchester, Coventry, Edinburgh, etc. And so on. In short, he conceives of the circumstance that it is raining in Birmingham as a constituent part of W_1, the total state of the world at t_1. W_1 could, in other words, be defined in terms of the truth values of all assertions which could be made about the world at t_1. Accordingly, to know the truth conditions of a declarative sentence could be defined as knowing the truth value of any assertion about the world made by using that sentence, relative to any value of W (W_1, W_2 . . . W_n), given a full specification of that value of W. In this way, under a truth-conditional semantic theory, adventitious ignorance about the world would not emerge as a defect in linguistic knowledge. Thus complete ignorance concerning meteorological conditions in Birmingham, past, present, or future, would not prevent someone from knowing the meaning of *It is raining in Birmingham.*

But a semantic theory which stopped short at the point just reached would have certain obvious limitations. While it would provide a basis for saying whether or not two declarative sentences had the same truth conditions, it would not appear to provide a basis for saying whether or not two sentences were synonymous, unless synonymy for declarative sentences were simply to be defined as identity of truth conditions. But this is hardly satisfactory, since two sentences might have identical truth conditions merely because no state of the world happened to be such that the corresponding assertions had different truth values. This would presumably be the case for, eg,

    (1) The first emperor of Rome was a Scythian

and   (2) The first emperor of Rome married Queen Victoria.

The example assumes, of course, that (a) the first emperor of Rome was not in fact a Scythian and did not in fact marry Queen Victoria, and (b) nothing in the past, present, or future history of the world can alter those facts. Both assumptions (a) and (b) seem to be reasonable. Assuming them to be correct, we should not wish to concede that (1) and (2) were synonymous, and a semantic theory which held that they were synonymous would *ipso facto* appear inadequate.

The move commonly made by truth-conditional theorists in order to circumvent limitations of this kind is to define truth conditions not by reference to all past, present and future states of the world in which we live, but by reference to 'all possible worlds'. The advantage of this neo-

Leibnizian strategy is intended to be that even if no state of the world we live in would justify the assignment of different truth conditions to sentences like (1) and (2), nonetheless it is possible to imagine that, had world history been different in certain respects, the first emperor of Rome might have been a Scythian, although not one who married Queen Victoria; or, alternatively, that Augustus, although not a Scythian, might have replaced Prince Albert. The two 'possible worlds' just described in part (PW_1 and PW_2) would both be worlds with respect to which the truth conditions of sentences (1) and (2) differed. So sentences (1) and (2) would not, according to this version of truth-conditional semantics, be synonymous.

If the strategy is to be acceptable, it needs to be clear on the one hand (i) that it does not impose requirements which have the result that any two sentences differing in form must automatically differ in meaning,[10] and on the other hand (ii) that it does not leave any residue of sentences which differ in meaning although not differing in truth conditions.

Assurance as to (i) will normally be provided by instancing pairs of declarative sentences which differ in form but nonetheless have identical truth conditions in all possible worlds. For example,

     (3) John looked up his old classmates

and   (4) John looked his old classmates up

will be considered to have identical truth conditions, unless it can be shown that it might conceivably be the case that John looked up his old classmates without looking them up. But this is not possible, since it requires that 'looking one's old classmates up' be envisaged as something other than 'looking up one's old classmates', which is tantamount to insisting that sentences (3) and (4) be treated not as sentences of current English, but as sentences of some imaginary language in which the position of the noun phrase *his old classmates* (or, equivalently, the position of *up*) will make a difference to the truth value of the corresponding assertions. Indeed, there might be such a language, but that is a possibility which does not affect the semantics of current English, which is deemed to be the language of sentences (3) and (4). So such a possibility does not invalidate the example,

---

[10] This is required in order to avoid commitment to the thesis that in the case of declarative sentences the 'synonymy postulate' does not hold for natural languages. There is, it will here be assumed, no good reason for accepting such a commitment. (For discussion, see R. Harris, *Synomymy and Linguistic Analysis* (Oxford: Blackwell, 1973), Introduction and Ch I.)

ie in any possible world describable in current English,[11] (3) and (4) have identical truth conditions. (To point out that there are possible worlds not describable in current English is doubtless correct, but irrelevant; as is also to point out that the sentences of current English might possibly have meant something different.)

Assurance as to (ii), however, is less easy to come by in view of the fact that natural languages afford the possibility of formulating sentences like

     (5) No triangle has more than three sides

and (6) No triangle has more than four sides.

Someone who makes an assertion using (5) is not saying the same thing about triangles as someone who makes an assertion using (6). Nonetheless, granted that *triangle* in both (5) and (6) is defined as, eg, 'three-sided plane figure', the two assertions will presumably have the same truth value not only in respect of any observed triangles but also in respect of any triangles in any possible world. For to anyone who claims that it is possible to have a world W_x in which triangles have just four sides, so that an assertion of the form (5) would be false for W_x, whereas an assertion of the form (6) would be true, it will be pointed out that this must involve either a contradiction or a redefinition of the term *triangle*. But any such redefinition is illicit in this context, while if W_x contains a logical inconsistency somewhere it is automatically not a 'possible world'.

What this shows is that the move to validate truth-conditional semantics by defining truth by reference to 'all possible worlds' will not work unless supplemented by a doctrine of substitutability of synonyms; eg the case of sentences like (5) and (6) can be saved on the ground that, although their truth conditions match, nonetheless the predicate expressions are not interchangeable in other sentences *salva veritate*. But there are two objections to this. One is that it is not clear that an appropriate doctrine of substitutability can be formulated without circularity.[12] For it would presumably be too strong a requirement to insist rigidly on interchangeability in all contexts. That would mean that even sentences like (3) and (4)

[11] To be more precise, describable in 'first-order current English', or 'current English without quotes', since the metalinguistic potential of natural languages will always make it possible, by incorporation of special stipulations concerning how certain expressions are to be understood in certain contexts, to describe a world in which the forms of current English are used in ways quite alien to the normal usage of current English.

[12] W. V. O. Quine, 'Two dogmas of empiricism', in Quine, *From a logical point of view* (2nd edn, Cambridge, Mass: Harvard UP, 1961).

failed to be synonymous, given that *look X up* and *look up X* are not interchangeable everywhere (cf *John looked up the chimney*). Secondly, whatever the precise formulation of the substitutability doctrine, it is clearly not derived from truth-conditional theory, but superimposed on it, since the defect it attempts to remedy is precisely that identity of truth conditions in all possible worlds does not provide an adequate explication of synonymity of declarative sentences. Thus it would be illusory to suppose that a truth-conditional definition of sentence-meanings supplies an independent basis on which one could then proceed to construct an account of the meanings of individual words.[13] Rather, it seems that the semantic role of individual words would have to be regarded as fixed independently of the truth conditions of sentences containing them, in order to support the truth-conditional account of sentence-meanings.

Even if an appropriate doctrine of substitutability were forthcoming, the neo-Leibnizian strategy is open to criticism on a further score. The concept of 'possible worlds' itself stands in need of clarification, for reasons which can be indicated by comparing eg *Triangles have four sides* with *Cats have eight legs*. Truth-conditional theory apparently predicts that *Triangles have four sides*, at least on one interpretation, is anomalous, the anomaly being a direct reflection of the logical impossibility of a plane figure which has three sides only, but a fourth side as well. Although a world which contained plane figures with merely unfamiliar but not logically incompatible characteristics would be a 'possible world', there is no such world containing four-sided triangles. The example is convincing in so far as we regard it as beyond dispute that this is a clear case of logical impossibility. But the case of *Cats have eight legs* is by no means straightforward. At first sight there seems to be no logical difficulty about the notion of a world identical to our own except for the fact that its cats have eight legs instead of four. Yet the question arises: are the 'cats' in this hypothetical world really cats? Or would not the correct description be that it has no cats (even though it has an otherwise unknown species of creatures which resemble cats in certain respects)? Here the recognition of a logical impossibility

---

[13] Exactly this advantage has been claimed for truth-conditional semantics, eg by Kempson, who proposes first to define sentence-meanings truth-conditionally and then 'define word meaning in terms of the systematic contribution a word makes to the interpretation of all sentences in which it occurs' (*op cit*, p 33). The paradoxical result of this would be that the words three and four would turn out to mean something different in sentences like (5) and (6) from what they mean in sentences like *Four is greater than three*.

seems to depend on the latitude of application we are prepared to tolerate for the term *cat*. But to concede this is already to begin to undermine the plausibility of the analysis. For unless it is in some way 'given' or established in advance which are 'possible worlds' and which are not, then the criterion of truth-conditional identity in 'all possible worlds' is deprived of its apparent uniformity and objectivity. Do we mean 'all possible possible worlds'? Or, if not, then 'possible' for whom? And under what conditions? As soon as truth conditions have to be relativized in this way, the attraction of appealing to 'the truth' vanishes. We are back with the familiar uncertainties of traditional semantics.

The uncertainties are in no way dispelled by consideration of the thought that whether one would be inclined to apply the term *cat* to a cat-like eight-legged species might depend to some extent on whether or not that species filled a gap in the ecology left by the absence of cats. This is to say, in a world in which these eight-legged creatures appeared INSTEAD OF cats, one might be more prepared to designate them by the term *cat* than in a world in which they appeared IN ADDITION TO cats. In the latter case perhaps it would seem more natural to treat them as non-cats than in the former case, where, in a sense, they would fulfil the role one has come to expect of cats. The point is that, according to the theory of truth-conditional semantics, this would make a difference to the meanings of sentences containing the word *cat*. So it is important to know whether one is being asked how one would describe such-and-such a phenomenon supposing it were taking the place of its familiar counterpart in the world of ordinary experience; or how one would describe it supposing it appeared alongside its familiar counterpart. Until it is stipulated exactly what the rules of the hypothetical-description game are, the concept of 'possible worlds' remains unclear.

However, an attempt to clarify it would hardly be worth the effort. For as soon as it becomes apparent that the question whether the world of eight-legged cats is a 'possible world', ie a world unmarred by logical inconsistency, resolves itself into the question whether *cat* is defined in such a way as to include or exclude application to this hypothetical species, it also becomes apparent that the question is irrelevant to the semantics of natural languages. For the linguistic contract between speakers of English which fixes the meanings of words like *cat* is not a contract intended to cover hypothetical language games of this kind. Whatever the meaning of the

English word *cat* is, one thing that is certain is that it has acquired — and maintains — that meaning in a world in which cats have four legs. How the word might be used if nature were different is doubtless an interesting speculation: but it is a speculation which has little to do with establishing the meaning of this or any other word in present-day English.

To ask what the semantic rules of a language are, given the situations the language has been evolved to deal with, is already a difficult enough question. To ask what they might be if the language were called upon to operate under quite different conditions is a question so much more difficult as to raise serious doubts whether it even makes sense. The programme implied by truth-conditional semantics amounts to proposing that we must somehow answer this latter question in order to answer the former: *obscurum per obscurius*.

Where does truth-conditional semantics go astray? That we recognize connexions between the truth of what a person says and what his words mean would be disputed by none but the most perverse of theorists. But somehow truth-conditional semantics misrepresents these connexions. If we are interested in analysing exactly how, we might perhaps begin by asking whether it is reasonable to suppose that such connexions as there may be between truth and linguistic meaning can in any case be handled in a uniform manner, by applying a single definitional formula, as truth-conditional theorists have proposed.

One reason for doubting this is that at least two types of case may be distinguished. If A and B are in agreement that the word *triangle* is to be defined as eg 'plane three-sided figure', then they do not need to find out in addition whether they agree that triangles in fact have three sides. Indeed, that question strictly does not arise, given their prior agreement upon the meaning of *triangle*. The agreement, at least as far as A and B are concerned, automatically guarantees the truth of the assertion 'Triangles have three sides'. But it does not similarly guarantee the truth of, eg, the assertion 'Triangles are unlucky'. In the case of the sentence *Triangles are unlucky*, granted that A and B agree on the meaning of *triangle* (as, eg, 'plane three-sided figure') and also on the meaning of *unlucky* (as, let us suppose, 'ill-omened'), there is still the question whether or not A and B agree that it is true that triangles are unlucky. Furthermore, on the basis of the assumptions just stated, there is no way that the agreement between A and B about the meaning of *Triangles are unlucky* is able to ensure their agreement about whether or not triangles are in fact unlucky. So the connexion between meaning and truth seems to be different in this case from that of *Triangles have three sides.*

Here the truth-conditional theorist may protest that precisely this difference is allowed for in truth-conditional semantics. For assertions of which the truth is, as it were, guaranteed by linguistic agreement, ie by the rules of the language, will turn out to be true always (true in all 'possible worlds'). Whereas there will be other cases in which an assertion is only sometimes true (true in some but not all 'possible worlds'). And this, he may plead, answers the objection.

But as far as the objector is concerned, a reply along these lines is likely to be taken not as answering but, on the contrary, as reinforcing the objection. The whole point, he will say, is that the distinction between 'always true' and 'sometimes true' is NOT an adequate interpretation of the difference between the two types of case. The difference relates to the kind of grounds on which a disagreement may arise, and hence to the nature of the agreement. It is this difference which explains how A and B can disagree about whether triangles are unlucky, even though they are entirely in agreement about the meaning of the sentence *Triangles are unlucky*. Speaker A may, for instance, think that B has simply got his facts wrong. Factual disagreements, in this sense, are different in kind from semantic disagreements. The difference is rather like the difference between arguing with a shopkeeper because you think there is a mistake in your bill, and arguing with him because you are not prepared to accept the prices he is charging you for the items you have purchased. (In the latter case, you should have settled the question of prices before entering into the transaction; but in commercial transactions, as in linguistic transactions, that sound advice is not — and cannot be — always followed.)

Truth-conditional semantics is committed to treating the two types of case alike, by admitting as characteristics of a possible world PW_x both 'linguistically guaranteeable' features, eg (a) that in PW_x triangles have three sides, and also 'linguistically non-guaranteeable' features, eg (b) that in PW_x it is raining in Birmingham. It is in this way tacitly assumed that (a) and (b) are comparable differentiae. But whereas rain in Birmingham may be a state of affairs in PW_x, the three-sidedness of triangles is not a state of affairs at all. It is simply a consequence of the linguistic stipulations, or general presuppositions, on the basis of which assertions about PW_x (and indefinitely many other 'worlds') rest. There is a category mistake here, concealed by the non-discriminatory use of 'true'. So long as 'true' is allowed to function as a catch-all term of approval, it conveniently disguises the problem of whether it makes sense to equate the two types of assertion, in one of which, but not the other, there is no risk of being proved wrong by the facts of the case. The problem is passed over in silence because treating the three-sidedness of triangles as a state of affairs, ie as being on a par with rain falling in Birmingham, or Smith's being hard of hearing, is technically essential for truth-conditional semantics. For if 'possible worlds' are regarded as differing from one another only in respect of the linguistically non-guaranteeable features, it becomes impossible to offer any plausible truth-based definition of synonymy at all.

But to explain what theoretical advantage is derived from this conflation is not to explain how it arises. The source can be traced right back to where truth-conditional semantics starts, ie with such seemingly innocuous and uncontroversial propositions as that someone 'makes a true statement if and only if things are as, in making that statement, he states them to be'.[14] Such a proposition already invites us to envisage truth as a matter of simple two-term correspondence between statements on the one hand and states of affairs on the other. The question 'From what point of view is the statement true?' receives no answer, because it is a question which is never allowed to arise. There is an implicit assumption that the viewpoint does not matter, or rather that there is some general, neutral viewpoint from which statements are true or otherwise. But this is not quite the way the concept of truth enters into our appraisal of what people say in everyday discourse. *True* is a word which is primarily used, as a metalinguistic predicate, either to express our agreement with someone else's assessment of a situation, or, somewhat differently, to make it clear that we do not think he is lying. It is the former type of case which is most directly relevant here. This use of *true* does not commit us to standing by what X said through thick and thin, come what may: it is essentially a context-bound judgement, in the sense that we thereby make no claim to have investigated every last shred of evidence before deciding whether or not to express our agreement with X's

[14] Strawson, *op cit*, p 15.

assessment, and rarely suppose that X has either. Our support is support for X's assessment IN A PARTICULAR COMMUNICATION SITUATION, ie relative to the tacitly understood purposes for which the communicational exchange takes place. It is evident that we cannot sensibly agree or disagree with what X says without understanding what his words mean; but it should be noted that all we need to understand for this is what point they have for purposes of that situation.

If Brown observes his wife about to go out and says, on looking out of the window, 'Take a coat. It's raining.', he should not be unduly perturbed if a Hollywood producer subsequently turns up on his doorstep and says: 'Well, I guess all you folks in this district thought it was raining; but it was really the Giant Panoramic Supersprinkler we're using to shoot a few wet scenes on location.' Not only was Brown's advice to his wife sensible, inasmuch as without a coat she would have got wet; but, furthermore, there is no reason at all for him to concede that what he said was not true. It is quite a different matter to ask him now to reassess the event in the light of the Hollywood producer's information and distinguish between natural and man-made downpours. Such a distinction was not in any way relevant to the original communication situation, although it is relevant *ex hypothesi* to the new one. We use declarative sentences in such ways as to draw just those distinctions which are relevant to the communication situation in hand. To suppose that we ought to use them more carefully or more accurately than this is to be a victim of philosophical pedantry in just the same way as to suppose that we ought not to end sentences with prepositions is to be a victim of grammatical pedantry.

Truth-conditional semantics in effect asks us to accept two overambitious idealizations. The first involves supposing that truth is not — or ought not to be — subject to contextual limitations, ie that there are 'absolute' criteria of assessment. The second involves supposing that these absolute criteria are what count in determining certain values for declarative sentences (their 'meanings') which are invariant as between all observable or conceivable speakers and circumstances. This would do no harm as an exercise in abstraction, if it were not then represented to us that using a natural language actually involves knowing these values determined by absolute truth-based criteria. Why this is unacceptable is that both idealizations are arrived at by abstraction from the communication situation and its particular function. The point can perhaps most succinctly be made in this way: there is no Universal Communication Situation with Universal Purposes. This is not to deny that it may sometimes be convenient to assume that there is, or could be: we may sometimes wish, as Austin put it, to 'aim at the ideal of what would be right to say in all circumstances, for any purpose, to any audience'.[15] But it is important to see that this aim will itself be relevant only in the context of a certain type of communication situation — one which is, no doubt, a rather special and infrequent type of communication situation. Austin did not make the mistake of supposing that natural languages ought to be regarded as being in some sense designed with just that aim in view.

The approach is not even one which has anything new to offer to linguistics; for what it offers has already been on offer before, in various forms. Bloomfield's theory of meaning was, in effect, a crude version of truth-conditional semantics. Bloomfield too held that the only way to define meanings was to state them by reference to what was true about the world. He would doubtless have approved the contention that one does not know what a declarative sentence means unless one knows under what conditions any assertion it is used to make is true. Where he went further than this was in not shrinking from the conclusion that accordingly, in some cases at least, no one knows what an expression means. (Thus whereas the meaning of *salt* could be defined, the meaning of *love* could not.) Semantics, therefore, could not be seriously undertaken 'until human knowledge advances very far beyond its present state'.[16] This is just one step short of the position taken by those logical positivists for whom any unverifiable assertion was meaningless. (Hence natural languages were characterized by the curious feature of having many sentences which existed, apparently, solely for the purpose of making meaningless assertions.)

In all these cases we are dealing with the same underlying view of how languages work: it is the view that languages are primarily nomenclatures. Hence whatever is designated by an expression is the meaning of that expression.[17] In the case of truth-conditional semantics, declarative

[15] J. L. Austin, *How to do things with words* (Oxford: Clarendon Press, 1962), p 145.
[16] L. Bloomfield, *Language* (London: Allen and Unwin, 1935), p 140.
[17] L. Wittgenstein, *Philosophische Unterxuchungen* (Oxford: Blackwell, 1953), p 2.

sentences are treated as designations of actual or possible states of affairs.[18] Hence to know what a declarative sentence means is to know what actual or possible state of affairs it designates, ie to know what would count as an instance of such a state of affairs (an instance in which the sentence could be used to make a true assertion) and what would not.

Why this will not do as a basis for natural language semantics is that, strictly interpreted, it is tantamount to claiming either that one must be omniscient in order to be a fully competent speaker of a natural language, or else that there may be sentences of which fully competent speakers do not understand the meanings.

Can we not, then, construct a more modest truth-conditional semantics, without the overambitious idealizations which preclude taking it seriously as an account of sentence-meanings in natural languages? By all means. But as soon as allowance is made for the practical limitations of speakers' knowledge and interests, it becomes necessary to begin replacing or supplementing the term 'true' by more cautious expressions like 'believed to be true', 'assumed to be justified', 'taken as correct', 'not usually dissented from', and to add circumstantial qualifications such as 'in this context' and 'for these purposes'. Any move to salvage truth-conditional semantics in this way compromises its distinctiveness as a theory of meaning, by introducing one or more of a variety of psychological notions which are themselves dependent in various ways on our understanding of communicational processes. But as soon as this happens, whatever the attempt to explicate meaning in terms of truth gains in credibility it immediately loses through obscurity. For what now stands in need of explication in addition to the communicational concept of meaning is the new communicational concept of truth.

---

[18] This is perhaps most explicit in Tarski, for whom the discipline of semantics 'deals with certain relations between the expressions of a language and the objects (or "states of affairs") "referred to" by those expressions' (A. Tarski, 'The semantic conception of truth', *Philosophy and Phenomenological Research* 4 (1944), pp 341–75 (p 345)).

Leo Spitzer's and Stephen Ullmann's Stylistic Criticism

HELMUT A. HATZFELD†

The Catholic University of America

Writing as a lifelong companion of the efforts of Leo Spitzer and as a close observer of the stylistic activities of Stephen Ullmann, and also, alas, as his much older survivor, I thought that I should not use secondary critical studies, with the exception of two excellent ones which envisage our two authors as critics. I am thinking of the study by René Wellek, 'Leo Spitzer (1887–1960)',[1] and the article by Lionello Sozzi, 'L'opera critica di Stephen Ullmann (1914–1976)'.[2] I found the two stylisticians, Spitzer and Ullmann, together for the first and the last time at the eighth Congress of the Fédération internationale des Langues et Littératures modernes, Liège, 1960, where Spitzer gave a survey in retrospect of his type of stylistic criticism under the title: 'Les Etudes de style et les différents pays',[3] while Ullmann presented the results of his then already remarkable work under the title: 'L'Image littéraire. Quelques questions de méthode'.[4] Spitzer's tone was pessimistic, his own stylistic criticism appearing to him merely as an episode in the history of criticism. He saw that it was time to make room for the ideals of another generation. That paper, delivered on 3 September 1960, was Spitzer's swan song, for he died on 16 September 1960. Ullmann's tone, by contrast, was optimistic: stylistic criticism, particularly

---

† The editors record with sorrow the death of Professor Helmut Hatzfeld while the present volume was in preparation. They understand from Professor John A. Frey of the Catholic University that this article was the last piece of scholarly work Professor Hatzfeld was able to complete.

[1] René Wellek, *Discriminations* (Yale University Press, 1970), pp 187–224.

[2] *Critica e storia letteraria. Studi offerti a Mario Fubini* (Padua: Liviana Editrice, 1970), pp 863–79.

[3] *Langue et Littérature. Actes du VIIIᵉ Congrès de la Fédération internationale des Langues et Littératures modernes* (Paris: Belles Lettres, 1961), pp 23–40.

[4] *Ibid*, pp 41–60.

when based on imagery, is a criticism *sui generis* and thus valid. Ullmann had sixteen more years to prove it, particularly with his Proustian studies. The approach to Proust by our two critics, after a general confrontation of their methods, will therefore be the closest possibility for comparison.

Leo Spitzer. Speaking of Leo Spitzer's method or methods, it should be kept in mind that at his beginnings, around 1910, a stylistic method did not exist. He surprised his master, Wilhelm Meyer-Lübke, with the choice of his dissertation, 'Die Wortbildung als stilistisches Mittel exemplifiziert an Rabelais'.[5] Spitzer acknowledged, still after half a century, the tolerance of Meyer-Lübke who had stated that he would leave stylistic studies to others: 'Quel émouvant exemple de modestie et de clairvoyance de la part d'un grand savant, grand aussi par la connaissance de ses limites'.[6] Spitzer's critics habitually regarded him as a pupil of Karl Vossler, and Spitzer always protested against this assumption. Vossler (1872–1949) in 1910 was only starting his own stylistic studies; his decisive publications were not yet known to Spitzer. Later he did share Vossler's idealistic approach, but in a most independent way. The greater event of the Geneva School, Charles Bally's type of stylistics, and even the posthumously published lectures of Ferdinand de Saussure were either unknown to or rejected by the young Spitzer. He actually seems to have been a self-made stylistician.

   He underwent, however, at the University of Vienna, a non-philological influence, namely that of the psychoanalysis of Sigmund Freud. Spitzer's Freudian analogy, which he later recognized as an error, replaced the problem of the disturbed psyche by that of the affective centre in the work of an exceptional author, who would reveal himself through his language. This method supposes, among other things, that the purpose of style criticism is to bare the soul of a writer. We owe, however, to Spitzer's *felix culpa* between 1910 and 1925, some very interesting studies on Charles-Louis Philippe, Henri Barbusse, Charles Péguy, Jules Romains, and Marcel Proust.

   Around 1925 Spitzer renounced any psychologism in style studies. At this point he probably recognized as superior to his own the method of Vossler which the latter was applying to more classical authors, such as

[5] *Beihefte zur Zeitschrift für Romanische Philologie*, No 19 (Halle, 1910).
[6] L. Spitzer, *Langue et Littérature*, p 24.

Dante, La Fontaine, Racine. He now understood that the very task of the stylistic critic is to discover the aesthetic tendencies in a literary work of art.[7] He proved his new viewpoint splendidly by an analysis of the badly misunderstood 'Consolation à Monsieur Du Périer'.[8] He discovered that the oft quoted text: 'Rose elle a vécu ce que vivent les roses . . .' was not an isolated line but, as one would say today, a pattern which emerges at different times in the poem, and which comes to its culmination in the final lines: 'Vouloir ce que Dieu veut, est la seule science/Qui nous met en repos.' Spitzer was not aware that he belonged to the generation of configurational psychology, and that he had discovered the *Gestalt* of the 'Consolation'. Later, however, he joked that he was already a structuralist.

Working for the first time with French Classicism, Spitzer understood the relationship of a particularly gifted poet to a highly organized and refined society with literary rules to be observed. The author as such is diminished in importance; the problem rather was to deliver quality and superiority within the limited liberties of a semantic–syntactical system. It is from this insight that Spitzer wrote 'Die Klassische Dämpfung in Racines Stil'.[9] Here Spitzer demonstrates, by artistically used linguistic material, the classicism of Racine's tragedies. The heroes do not possess any idiosyncratic eccentricity. They speak always with dignity, whether in sinful or in heroic situations. The hateful *moi* is replaced by the proper name; the sign of modesty is counterbalanced by the sign of solemnity in the form of the *pluralis majestatis*. Statements are supposed to have universal validity, and are earmarked by the indefinite article. Superlative expressions are toned down by *si* and *tant* instead of *très* and *beaucoup*. Stephen Ullmann called this article of Spitzer '. . . a spectacular demonstration'.[10]

Spitzer, the pragmatic genius in stylistics, having reached such heights of achievement, then tried a theoretical justification of his method, an action which aroused the antagonism, if not the hostility, of his adversaries. His theory is found in condensed form in his book *Linguistics and Literary History*.[11] Herein he mixes up his 'Freudian' and his 'Vosslerian' method, ie

[7] *Ibid*, p 28.
[8] 'Ehrenrettung von Malherbes "Consolation à Monsieur Du Périer"', *Stilstudien II. Stilsprachen* (Munich: Max Hueber, 1928), pp 18–29.
[9] L. Spitzer, *Romanische Stil- und Literaturstudien I* (Marburg: Elwert, 1931), pp 135–268.
[10] S. Ullmann, *Meaning and Style* (Oxford: Blackwell, 1973), p 88.
[11] L. Spitzer, *Linguistics and Literary History. Essays in Stylistics* (Princeton: University Press, 1948), pp 1–39.

his search for the author, and his search for the aesthetic centre of the text. One of the best essays in this regard in the collection is 'The Style of Diderot'.[12] Spitzer avows, however, that he had used in all of his examples Schleiermacher's so-called philological circle. He is fascinated by Schleiermacher's comparative *and* divinatory method. The latter concept gives him the assurance that intuition, identified by him with something mysterious and metaphysical, must be the first condition of the stylistic critic, before discovering, after reading and re-reading a poem, or novel, or drama, concrete stylistic details.[13] From the single elements the stylistician finds his way to the overall structure of the work, and then back again to similar, single supporting features. Even if Spitzer's own interpretation of his 'circle' be wrong, it still may be said that his cultural knowledge and sensitivity to a literary text give him the impressionistic possibility of making a scholarly hypothesis about the whole, whereupon he then seeks corresponding details which may seem reasonable, if the first supposition was correct.[14] Offering a kind of *hysteron proteron* in his interpretation, Spitzer evidently was not aware that he belonged, as mentioned earlier, to the then upcoming generation of configurational psychology which maintained a symphonic view on wholes in which each detail has its place with regard to the entire work. It could also be said that Spitzer unconsciously follows a sound hermeneutics in which his own broad education, erudition and historical consciousness are included. From this he then works outwards in all directions.[15]

It was a very great disappointment for Spitzer, however, that scholars would not accept as a method worthy of discussion what he had called the stylistic circle or the to-and-fro movement. Eager since his first work to see stylistic forms as direct expressions of ideologies, he begins to shift his interest more and more to ideological and historical themes. If he then speaks of 'historical semantics', it is only a terminology to keep such studies within the boundaries of linguistics, and as such has nothing to do with technical semasiological penetrations in the sense of Ullmann. In his

[12] *Ibid*, pp 135–92.

[13] *Ibid*, p 33, note 10.

[14] John M. Ellis, 'Critical Interpretation, Stylistic Analysis and Logic of Inquiry', *Journal of Aesthetics and Art Criticism* (Spring, 1978), pp 253–62, p 255.

[15] See Jean Starobinski, 'Leo Spitzer et la stylistique', in his translated selections of Spitzer's articles: *Les Etudes de style par Leo Spitzer* (Paris: Gallimard, 1970), pp 8–40.

volume of collected essays 1936–56 the new trend becomes evident. Spitzer becomes interested, for example, in Joachim Du Bellay's sonnet *Si notre vie est moins qu'une journée*. He knows that it is a translation, almost a literal one, from a minor Italian poet. But on the basis of some slight technical or perhaps emotional changes in Du Bellay's translation of the Italian text, Spitzer detects in the French poet's work an intense desire for Heaven or the Platonic world of ideas, where the poet may find love, peace and bliss.[16] After some revamping in the periodical *Traditio*, this stylistic study became a full-fledged ideological treatise in book form.[17] The Italian translation of this book even carries the sub-title: 'Storia semantica di un' idea'.[18]

It would be wrong, however, to explain Spitzer's personal stylistic defeatism as a disenchantment with his own methods. For his genius the field was simply too narrow; he had already written in 1931:

> Ich beabsichtige meinerseits nach besten Kräften dahinzuwirken, dass die Stilistik als autonomer Zweig der Sprachwissenschaft, nachdem ich ihn jahrelang gepflegt, verschwinde und in der *einen* Literaturwissenschaft, von der er sich abgespalten hat, wieder aufgehe.[19]

One year before his death he made the following statement:

> In bezug auf die angewandeten literaturwissenschaftlichen Methoden huldige ich mit fortschreitendem Alter mehr und mehr einem Eklektizismus, der um der vorherrschenden Bemühung (der stilistischen) willen andere Betrachtungsweisen . . . nicht ausschliesst.[20]

What Spitzer tried to achieve was an overall criticism through language. René Wellek has well seen that Spitzer's criticism, seeking to establish a general evaluation, simply could not be limited to either aesthetic or linguistic analysis.[21]

---

[16] 'The Poetic Treatment of a Platonic-Christian Theme', *Romanische Literaturstudien 1936–1956* (Tübingen: Niemeyer, 1959), pp 130–59.

[17] *Classical and Christian Ideas of World Harmony. Prolegomena to an Interpretation of the Word Stimmung*, ed Anna Granville Hatcher (Baltimore: The Johns Hopkins University Press, 1963).

[18] *L'armonia del mondo* (Bologna, 1967).

[19] *Romanische Stil- und Literaturstudien*, p 30.

[20] *Romanische Literaturstudien 1936–1956*, p 5.

[21] René Wellek, *op cit*, p 200.

In all his stages, however, Spitzer explored the stylistic side of literature, if only as a springboard to a higher type of criticism of which he was also a master. To adopt the words of his not uncritical admirer, Stephen Ullmann:

> The great merit of Spitzer's procedure is indeed that it has lifted stylistic facts out of their isolation and has related them to other aspects of the writer's experience and activity.[22]

This may suffice to characterize *in general* Spitzer as a stylistic critic.

Stephen Ullmann.   Stephen Ullman's stylistic criticism consistently affirms the serious principle that stylistics is a specific aspect of linguistics in which, in the sense of Bally, Brunot, Marouzeau, and Cressot, the facts must be first rigorously established. It is only then that a limited intuition may be brought to bear upon the interpretation, while always remaining of course within the aesthetic limits.[23] Not sharply separating *langue* and *parole* so as not to destroy any historical-synchronic unit through systematization, Ullmann declares his stylistics to be '. . . not a mere branch of linguistics but a parallel discipline which investigates the same phenomena from its own point of view'.[24] As a representative of the new generation Ullmann knows much more than Spitzer about structuralism, and consequently has in mind a more radical sense of the whole than Spitzer when he studies the metaphorical elements in the imagery of a work of art. He keeps, however, a safe distance from the amateurish structuralism of Paris.[25] He concentrates on imagery as a necessary creation for what would otherwise be inexpressible in literary language, and he finds confirmation of his opinion in the theory and practice of those authors whom he treats. Metaphorical elements appear as highlights between many other paradigmatic and syntactical elements recognized as colourful in themselves and functional for the entire work. Ullmann's intentionally restricted criticism operates within these

---

[22] S. Ullmann, *Style in the French Novel* (Cambridge University Press, 1957), p 29.

[23] S. Ullmann, *Language and Style* (Oxford: Blackwell, 1964), p 155.

[24] S. Ullmann, 'Stylistics and Semantics', in *Meaning and Style* (Oxford: Blackwell, 1973), pp 41–63.

[25] Cf Georges Mounin, *Clefs pour la linguistique* (Paris: Seghers, 1968), and Robert Hall's review of Lothard Fietz, *Funktionaler Strukturalismus*, 1976, in *The Western Humanities Review*, 32 (1978), p 185.

limits. If Ullmann's domain were as wide as Spitzer's, imagery as principle would perhaps only be valid for the modern novel. Here however, with some exceptions, it is the most fruitful approach, and this conviction is shared with Ullmann by the whole Anglo-Saxon world, and by scholarly research:

> The high esteem in which the image is held by most writers is matched by the prominent place it occupies in stylistic research. Not only is it the theme of countless special studies but it also has the lion's share in many monographs on the style of particular works or authors.[26]

Open to all ancillary, even statistical methods, Ullmann also considers their inability to cope with overlapping and interlocked images.[27] Ullmann never tries, as does Spitzer, to extend his stylistic criticism into a general evaluation. He sees clearly:

> If one is thinking in terms of value judgements, then it cannot be denied that some outstanding novelists are indifferent stylists. Balzac's style had many flaws, Zola wrote, as André Gide once put it, with a badly sharpened pencil, and other examples come readily to one's mind.[28]

Once he has got an overall view of a work, and preparatory to his study of imagery, Ullmann starts with small units, generally something which would be strikingly concrete for the semanticist, and which becomes of interest to the stylistician in its contextual analysis, and to the critic in its operational function. It is thus that he finds the key to the art of the Goncourt brothers in their nominal style where adjectives and abstracts assume the function of concrete action, with attempts at eliminating the verb. In this manner he makes *style indirect libre* the proof of the objective-subjective action of *Madame Bovary*.[29] He finds impressionistic style most adequately utilized by Mme de Noailles.[30] All of these style elements are scrutinized as stepping-stones to metaphor and imagery, according to the role they play: operational, parasitic, anecdotic, euphonic, rhythmic, affective; the

---

[26] S. Ullmann, *Language and Style*, p 175.

[27] *Ibid*, p 119.

[28] *Style in the French Novel*, p 260.

[29] *Meaning and Style*, pp 3–5.

[30] *Ibid*, p 147.

metaphors themselves are viewed as original, revitalized, precise, ambiguous, poetical, ironical.

Much stylistic criticism is already certain to be found in the observation of the individual metaphors in the single novels. Ullmann states for instance that, if the imagery representing the forces of nature in Giono's *Regain* has no wide range, these metaphors are yet redeemed by their authenticity;[31] Sartre's two hundred and fifty animal and insect images, while perhaps personifying anguish, remain helplessly in the intellectual sphere and represent '. . . concentrated vulgarity and obscenity'.[32] This judgement is meant as an aesthetic appraisal based on language.

Ullmann may have sinned by overdoing his imagistic principle, ie by forcing the well-known representatives of the *écriture-zéro* to fit his metaphorical bed of Procrustes. Thus he goes through the entire work of André Gide without finding any remarkable analogies.[33] Yet he discovers that symbolic tendencies in Gide cannot do without striking imagery as in *Les Nourritures terrestres, La Porte étroite, La Symphonie pastorale,* and *Les Faux-Monnayeurs.* In Camus he has discovered the most diversified use and distribution of images, according to the type of narrative. A hidden political symbolism permeates *La Peste.*[34] In *L'Etranger* the main image is reserved for the murder of the Arab where reality and hallucination fuse in the mind of Meursault under the burning desert sun. Here the image contains the motivation of the plot.[35] So much about the *general* approach of Ullmann.

Spitzer's Proust Study. Among Spitzer's many studies, not one seems closer to his heart and mind than the analysis of Proust's novel, *Du Côté de chez Swann.*[36] I shall try to digest, translate and comment the 132 pages, following closely Spitzer's text and condensing it. Spitzer begins with what is to him the most striking phenomenon, namely the sentence structure. He does not, however, consider such syntactical details as inversion and other changes in word order, but rather the rhythm as it relates to the different

---

[31] *Style in the French Novel,* p 225.
[32] *Ibid,* p 257.
[33] *The Image in the Modern French Novel* (Cambridge University Press, 1960), p 97.
[34] *Language and Style,* p 194.
[35] *Ibid,* p 195.
[36] 'Zum Stil Marcel Prousts', in *Stilstudien II. Stilsprachen,* pp 365–497.

meanings of the sentences. This procedure gives us a clear insight into Spitzer's manner of working. The Proustian sentence is complicated because Proust's thought and life are complicated. But his sentence has a pattern, eg in the *Mäandermuster* of a bifurcation with two parentheses. Now, the new mentalistic explication becomes more difficult, but Spitzer dares say that despite all insertions, 'an immense calm' comes from such sentences. Not everybody will see it that way. Spitzer the syntactician becomes the victim of the subject matter. When he encounters a sentence ending in a negatively so-called *cadence mineure*, covering the description of a fountain: '. . . la jolie forme, où il y avait une chute d'eau', he finds that 'une chute d'eau' makes a charming 'chute de la phrase'. Another example where subject matter ignores the syntactical meaning is the statement that if feminine gracefulness is described, the sentence ends with a 'geste d'abandon', while in other cases it ends with a 'détonation'. Metaphors are seen as elements of preparation, suspense, surprise, like the maritime flowers preparing the landscape for the appearance of the sea: *Thalatta*, la mer. More eerie manifestations, noises at the window, the sight of the village steeple in the dark, are underlined with :'C'était la pluie, le doigt de Dieu'.

Still working with the same elements, parenthesis and bifurcation, Spitzer now goes into the details of their structure and into the means of binding together the diffuse parts of these overfraught sentences. But the problem truly involves the background of the devices he is discussing. What is the meaning on the psychological level of the parenthesis? Helplessness in the face of life's complexities, according to Spitzer. On the artistic level, to this blowing up on the sentence level corresponds a blowing up of the total organization of the first book of Proust's novel. This, however, seems doubtful since the book was meant by Proust to be reorganized. Theoretically the parentheses are said to contain the exterior facts of astronomical time, while the main clauses contain the concerns of the spirit and of *durée*. This last generalization also decides the role of the parenthesis as a larger compositional element: it is a point from which the author looks at his actions and at his readers.

The two arms of bifurcation of the sentence serve as exemplary oppositions, eg the lovesick behaviour of Swann '. . . comme un mor-phinomane ou un tuberculeux'. Such original disjunctions are continued, with distinctions introduced by *non pas — mais, sinon — du moins*, etc.

According to Spitzer these syntactical devices express the desire for the 'vraie vie' in the midst of the calm of a sage. If the contradictions cannot be resolved, Spitzer continues, they prove the ironical-suffering attitude of Proust. Again Spitzer is more interested in the interpretation of the linguistic expression than in any thorough-going analysis.

After isolating all the disjunctions and distinctions of the Proustian sentence, Spitzer looks out for linkages which often seem rather hidden. But he finds them first in the adjectival or participial anticipation of a later-appearing important substantive as heralding the sentence: 'Emportée par le vol de deux chevaux je voyais . . . une incomparable victoria'; secondly, in temporal clauses closely knitted together by their formulation as consecutive clauses introduced by *si que, tellement que*; thirdly, in the *style indirect libre*, in which thoughts and words of author and fictional persons are fused and interwoven.

All the other stylistic remarks are interesting in themselves, but they are not systematically assembled. Spitzer makes bold to observe sound effects, intonation, and gestures accompanying the speech of individual characters. Proust's tendency to quote directly is for him a sign of avoiding responsibility. The name of Swann allegedly represents for a French ear, elegance and music. The symbolic expression, 'faire cattleya' for the sexual love of Swann and Odette, with allusion to the orchids she wore at her first surrender, is stressed by Spitzer as a leitmotif. If a residence in the city of Parma is called '. . . une demeure lisse, mauve et douce', he suspects, behind this expression, the reminiscence of an advertisement for a perfume called 'violette de Parme'. Spitzer's speculations become more philosophical when he supposes Proust's inexhaustible use of the prefix *in* to be a quest for immortality through art: *impalpable, immatériel, ineffable, inépuisable, inaccessible, invisible, introuvable*. This identification of immortality with the involuntary resurgence of a transfigured past is said to be marked by the prefix *re*: *reconnaître, retrouver, recréer, reconquérir, récupérer, remettre*.

The mystery of the narrator behind an ambiguous 'je' has allegedly a parallel in the frequent 'comme si' referring to the fictional experiences, and the no less frequent 'peut-être', explaining possible psychologies behind actions. Spitzer feels entitled to attribute to Proust a 'que sais-je?' attitude, due to the impressionistically assessed frequency of the verbs *sembler, paraître, avoir l'air, soupçonner*. Proust's notorious irony sometimes eludes Spitzer. For instance, the comparison of the maid Françoise selecting meat at the market with Michelangelo selecting the most perfect marble for the tomb of Pope Julius II is explained by Spitzer as a re-establishment of original hierarchies which have been destroyed by the artificiality of our civilization. He still tries to explain Proust's famous interlocking of two comparisons as a glance into one experience from two levels. In similar fashion the philosophical and didactic parts are constantly and smoothly fused with the narrative sections. For Spitzer this means: 'The monumental and eternal element gives importance to the temporal and specific.'

Spitzer was well aware that he had only dealt with one aspect of the style of Proust in the first two volumes of his great novel, and consequently had not covered the style in its entirety. And the brilliance of his formulations may make the analysis of the sentence appear more important for the whole than it really is. Spitzer's analysis belongs to the very early stages of Proust studies, the only predecessors in 1928 being Ernst Robert Curtius, Léon Pierre-Quint and Benjamin Crémieux. When I read Spitzer's essay for the first time a half-century ago, I found it fascinating. Re-reading it today I am disturbed by two things: first, by the importance which Spitzer gives to the *beau désordre* of the Proustian sentence, treating figures of speech in a rather perfunctory manner; second, by a rather lofty criticism which the casual or non-preoccupied reader would not be able to derive from the examples cited. Stylistic observation and analysis, selective and incomplete as they may be, show Spitzer's real strength; his critical conclusions, however, one suspects, are not dependent upon the examples analysed.

Ullmann's Proust Study. Ullmann uses the same two Swann volumes as material, but declares as his aim, 'The Metaphorical Texture of a Proustian Novel'. I digest his 115 pages following closely the text. Ullmann[37] offers a critical selection of metaphors from a near complete inventory. He uses as yardsticks the '. . . impressions profondes et esthétiques', a viewpoint which is certainly justified since the awareness or recognition of striking analogies is '. . . at the root of aesthetic enjoyment'. In the descriptive part alone Ullmann counts seven hundred and fifty images. Like Spitzer, he too thinks of the personality of Marcel Proust as a link to these images, but unlike Spitzer, he does not construct a psychogram. Rather he bears in

---

[37] *The Image in the Modern French Novel*, pp 124–238.

mind that Proust was a lifelong invalid who was also the son and brother of
medical doctors. Ullmann sees this medical background as the reason for
the overdone nosographic images. In this connection he cites Spitzer's
example of the doubly lovesick Swann as *tuberculeux* and *morphinomane*,
showing, however, that '. . . au fur et à mesure que grandissait la
souffrance, grandissait en même temps le prix du calmant'. The extreme
correctness of some of the medical images justifies their strangeness, eg the
to-and-fro movement of the water-lilies likened to the neurasthenic
restlessness of aunt Léonie. Ullmann registers dissatisfaction with these
medical images, however, because of their unpleasant flavour and morbid
effect which, for him, block aesthetic enjoyment. Structurally, on the other
hand, when seen together with Proust's scientific images, they are witness
to Proust's objectivity, which Spitzer identifies as the attitude of the sage.
The most important scientific analogy concerns of course the quintessence
of the novel: time and memory. Proust conceives of '. . . un espace de
quatre dimensions, la quatrième étant celle du Temps'. The passing of
time which appears so differently to composed and to excited characters is
likened to slow and fast speeds in automobiles. Memories are said to be
'. . . des gisements précieux dans le riche bassin minier du cerveau'. The
memories of Combray are in the deepest subsoil of the narrator's mind. To
the passions scientifically studied at length throughout the novel belongs
jealousy (Swann-Odette, Marcel-Albertine). Jealousy is compared to the
selfish and voracious vitality of the octopus '. . . qui jette une première,
puis une seconde, puis une troisième amarre'. There are many other
scientific images, the better ones striking Ullmann by their precision, their
elegance, and their wide angle, according to the terminology of Richard A.
Sayce, between tenor and vehicle.

In his very fine survey of the better known art analogies, Ullmann
reminds us that they only make sense to the culturally prepared reader who
may be able to see, together with Swann, his Odette as the Zephora in
Botticelli's fresco in the Sistine Chapel. Distasteful persons in life appear
enhanced in dignity when compared to figures in paintings, Bloch
compared to one in a painting of Bellini, Swann to one of the magi of Luini,
Charlus to the Grand Inquisitor of El Greco. It becomes more difficult to
compare 'la petite phrase de Vinteuil' with the particular perspective of
Pieter de Hooch. Not quite clearly seen by Ullmann is the supplementation
of a metaphor under a synecdochical contact influence, for instance the

appearance of the steeple of Combray viewed from the baker's shop as a huge loaf of bread. Metonymies such as these were systematized by Gérald Genette who credits Ullmann, however, with having discovered the problem.[38] If a steeple is seen between houses in a seaside town in Normandy, it appears like a seashell caught between two pebbles.

The metaphorical effects of musical preoccupations are pertinently stressed. Their strangeness does not impair their impressiveness. The sun '. . . dont le couchant n'éclairait plus que le faîte' is compared to '. . . un chant repris en voix de tête une octave au-dessus'. The beautiful red hawthorn of Tansonville, found among the many white ones, is likened to a piano piece clothed in the colours of an orchestra. It must be said at this point that Ullmann never forgets to make some general stylistic-syntactical remarks on the forms in which this and other images appear, thus covering the same territory which had originally interested Spitzer. The peak of the musical imagery is 'la petite phrase de Vinteuil', already mentioned, which accompanies the unfolding of Swann's love. It first appears as a simple sonata for piano and violin, and finally is heard as a full orchestral performance, compared respectively to the encounter with a beautiful woman in the street and to the solemn introduction to her in the drawing room.

In contradistinction to Spitzer, Ullmann studies the Swann volumes in their relation to the entire novel. He pays attention therefore to the relationship between young girls and flowers which culminates in the volume 'A l'ombre des jeunes filles en fleurs'. From the very beginning, as Ullmann has well seen, the young girl is considered as a naturally growing plant belonging to the landscape, a case in point being the hawthorns of Tansonville. The white ones are simple, like girls in their négligés, but the outstanding red tree is comparable to a girl festively dressed up: 'Une jeune fille en robe de fête . . . tel brillait en souriant dans sa fraîche toilette rose l'arbuste catholique et délicieux'. The sentimental comparison does not impede the hawthorn's 'catholique' destiny as decoration for the May altar and for the repositories of the Corpus Christi procession. For this reason the whole hedge is seen as a '. . . suite de chapelles'. This method, which is not overstressed by Ullmann, consists in the fusion of the sacred and the erotic image and vice versa. Thus it is said of the church in

---

[38] Gérald Genette, 'Métonymie chez Proust', in his *Figures, III* (Paris: Seuil, 1972), pp 41–63.

Combray that the first Gothic arcades seem to hide the rough Romanesque structure '. . . comme de plus grandes sœurs, pour le cacher aux étrangers, se placent en souriant devant un jeune frère rustre, grognon et mal vêtu'.

Besides such personifications, the concretizations often reach a stage of hallucination, and appear very Rabelaisian, when, eg, the fire in Aunt Léonie's rooms '. . . cuisant comme une pâte les appétissantes odeurs . . . les feuilletait, les dorait, les godait, les boursouflait . . .'. Another example is that of a sleeper in a well-heated room who feels as though he is '. . . dans un grand manteau d'air chaud, sorte d'impalpable alcôve, de chaude caverne, de zone ardente'.

Ullmann sees how the hallucinatory images form a type. The madeleine which evokes, luminous in the darkness of a slow awakening, the childhood tragedy of the maternal goodnight kiss, and all of the memories of Combray, or the sound of the bells of Saint-Hilaire, which provoke the daydreaming narrator, reading in the garden, to '. . . voir tomber morceau par morceau ce qui de l'après-midi était déjà consommé'. The interior of Swann literally freezes to ice because of an offending word of Odette which '. . . comme un morceau de glace, l'immobilisait, durcissait sa fluidité, le faisait geler tout entier'.

Like Spitzer, the language-minded and linguistically very competent Ullmann also chooses other aspects of Proustian speech for consideration, namely the dialogue behaviour of the speakers, emanating from their emotions and passions. The well-educated Swann loses all restraint upon learning that Odette frequents the same summer resort as the Verdurins, and in his rage shouts: '. . . villégiatures dans les latrines pour être plus à portée de respirer des excréments'. Mme Verdurin and Odette show their lack of education by constantly employing stock metaphorical locutions. Dr Cottard is eager to use correct idioms; Professor Brichot is a devotee of historical analogies; Bloch has the speech of a vulgar dandy, peppered with classical school reminiscences; Legrandin speaks in a stilted but erudite manner, with bookish and over-refined imagery.

We may ask what has been achieved by the Proust analysis of Ullmann? Although he clung exclusively to the study of imagery, he did cover by this special approach all of the stylistic implications which Spitzer had tried to isolate, word order, rhythm, figures of *speech* as different from the studied figures of *thought*. He perceived the sharp differences between the narrative, the didactic and the dialogued text, differences of which Spitzer seems to have been unaware. The qualification of the characters by metaphorically diversified speech was a particular discovery of Ullmann. This method leads intrinsically to a systematic presentation. The essential style situation of the Swann volumes has been correctly assessed through imagery. The same cannot be said for Spitzer's sentence analysis. If Spitzer's sometimes beguiling intuitive interpretations are missing from Ullmann's work, the latter's more factual interpretations are more verifiable, and thus more convincing.

Comparison: A general comparison of these two stylistic criticisms leads to the conclusion that Spitzer's approach presupposes a kind of genius, a particular intuitive grasp of the text upon which any research is dependent, while Ullmann proposes a well-controlled analysis equipped with the ordinary philological tools available to everyone. Spitzer seeks the striking, the exceptional, from which it is difficult to draw a synthesis; Ullmann looks for the characteristic of a work, from which will be assessed the importance and the choice of details, moving towards a systematization from the very inception of the work. Spitzer condemns any 'dénombrements', frequency lists, or exhaustive exemplifications as '. . . superposant à une œuvre poétique les casiers de la grammaire'. Ullmann, though far from recommending enumerations *per se*, is convinced that selective choices, without the control of the complete number of the respective devices, are meaningless for any serious conclusion. Stylistic criticism is to Spitzer — *incredibile dictu* — '. . . peut-être une activité passagère'; for Ullmann, the only possible scholarly criticism. Although both critics are text-minded philologists, linguists and semanticists, Spitzer is never satisfied with the merely aesthetic evaluation, and tries desperately for a way out or beyond this limitation. Ullmann, however, understands that the aesthetic criticism which results from the stylistic material is the only one for which the analyst can make himself responsible and feels competent. Spitzer is neither strong nor consistent in stylistic theory, while Ullmann offers well-elaborated theoretical considerations. On the other hand, Spitzer always tried, for each phenomenon or fact of style, to offer a psychological explanation based in the personality of the author. Ullmann refuses any interpretation which cannot be made evident to the reader. The range of Spitzer's stylistic investigation is very wide, comprising the literatures of France, Italy, Spain, Portugal, and Rumania, including all epochs from the Middle Ages to very modern times, encompassing all possible genres from the troubadour lyrics to the *nouveau roman.* Ullmann limited his activity to one aspect of the French sector, the novel of the nineteenth and twentieth centuries. Although his range is narrower, his results are more exact, and are generally acknowledged. Spitzer's criticism is frequently superimposed upon his stylistic findings, not emanating directly from the text. Ullmann's criticism remains inseparable from his analysis, its intrinsic *raison d'être*, its justification.

New Thoughts on Macro-Contact Studies

T. E. HOPE

Professor of French Language and Romance Philology, University of Leeds

It was perhaps as well, Stephen Ullmann once remarked, that the edition of his first book was almost totally destroyed in the London blitzes of 1940. 'It was not a work I am particularly proud of', he explained. His reservations, one should add, applied to the book's style and language, not to its matter. From that angle the criticism was not without foundation; it is true that some of the earliest works Ullmann published bear traces of the artificiality to be expected from one who acquired English as a foreign language, however talented its exponent might be. But as regards content and treatment *Europe's Debt to the English Language*[1] already displayed the masterly documentation that was Ullmann's hallmark, as well as a characteristic awareness of exactly what the book's purpose was to be and how that purpose could best be put across to his reader. In more ways than one it typifies the earlier, exploratory phase of his research, when he was interested almost exclusively in what we nowadays call interlanguage studies, or phenomena relating to contact between languages (which throughout the first half of this century meant almost exclusively phenomena exemplified with reference to items of borrowed vocabulary). Half-a-dozen of Ullmann's articles as well as a doctorate thesis remain to us from this period.[2] The approach of *Europe's Debt to the English Language* was

---

[1] *Europe's Debt to the English Language: A Study of the influence of English on Dutch, German, French and Italian* (London: Pilot Press, 1940), 154 pp.

[2] 'Hungarian Words in English', *Hungarian Quarterly* 4 (1939), pp 1–5; 'Note sur la chronologie des anglicismes en français classique et postclassique', *FM* 8 (1940), pp 345–9; 'The Rhythm of English Infiltration into Classical French', *ML* 23 (1941), pp 55–8; 'Types and Patterns of English Influence on the Languages of Western Europe', *ML* 24 (1942), pp 4–13; 'Anglicism and Anglophobia in Continental Literature', *ML* 27 (1945), pp 8–16, 47–50; 'Anglicisms in French: Notes on their Chronology, Range and Reception', *PMLA* 62 (1947), pp 1153–7. Doctorate Thesis: 'Italian Influences on the English Literary Language in the period of the Renaissance' (in Hungarian), *Studies in English Philology No 1* (1936) (Publication of the Royal Hungarian Péter Pazmány University, English Institute), pp 50–88.

E

innovatory, yet conventional at the same time. What was innovatory was the concept of linguistic diffusion in a context other than that of the classical languages. It was not, admittedly, the first book to compare the fortunes of a single cultural language in different environments. Paul Meyer did so with relation to Italian as early as 1906, and in the same area one recalls Vidos's impressively annotated essay *La forza di espansione della lingua italiana*, published in 1932.[3] But in 1940 (the date of Ullmann's book) the method was still largely untried, and the same is true of it today in the sense that the opportunities it offers have not been taken up seriously so far. Even more valuable than 'diffusion' as such, with its necessarily superficial connotation, is the contrastive/comparative element which diffusion implies, and which rests on the assumption that a given source language will give rise to interference patterns which differ according to the differing linguistic contexts into which it is introduced. I shall refer to this comparative aspect again later.

As might be expected, conventional standpoints current among lexicologists of the time can readily be identified in Ullmann's ill-fated *coup d'essai*, just as they can in the whole of the period when contact studies claimed his attention. This may be taken to extend from his earliest published work in 1936 to the immediate post-war years, let us say, up to 1949. Most of what he wrote followed in direct line the traditional 'cultural history through loan-words' monograph of the pre-Weinreich era; in other words the kind of lexicology upon which Els Oksaar poured scorn in her 1972 review of interlanguage research and methodology which appeared as a chapter of *Current Trends in Linguistics* volume IX (pp 476–511). So far as I know Ullmann never seriously doubted the theoretical validity or the scholarly respectability of a language and culture approach when it was based on lexical data cross-checked by sound etymological methods, and one must do him the justice of pointing out that none of his work in this field fell foul of the pitfalls into which Vossler and the other Idealist historians of language so easily stumbled. The concept of a *Zeitgeist* presiding over the fate of even the most immanent linguistic features, for instance. Ullmann's scholarship at all periods of his productive life was too

---

[3] Reprinted in B. E. Vidos, *Prestito, espansione e migrazione dei termini tecnici delle lingue romanze e non-romanze* (Florence: Olschki, 1965), pp 47–68. In spite of the book's title this chapter does not limit itself to technical vocabulary. See also Paul Meyer, *De l'expansion de la langue française en Italie pendant le moyen-âge, 12e–13e siècles* (Rome: R. Accad. dei Lincei, 1904).

rational, too coolly objective for such imaginative excesses. His level-headedness in the face of Vosslerian teleology is all the more admirable when one recalls that Idealism in itself was not repugnant to him and that one of Croce's most illustrious disciples, Leo Spitzer, exerted a profound influence upon Ullmann's choice of method and theme, especially where research in the domain of stylistics was concerned.

Looking back with the privilege of hindsight we can see that the nineteen-fifties were a decade of radical change in almost all aspects of lexicology, etymology and semantics. Of revolutionary change, even. The term is not too forceful to describe how so many assumptions which had been held as axiomatic for half a century were suddenly felt to be questionable and then, as interest shifted elsewhere, irrelevant. Traditional works on contacts between languages did not escape the general fault-finding. The critical process followed a recognizable pattern. Individual details of methods used or inferences drawn were analysed, examined and found wanting; consequently the lexical exercise of which they were a part was judged to be unsafe, mentalistic, unscientific. Yet one trait — probably the one which most clearly typifies these traditional interlanguage investigations — seems largely to have gone unnoticed, perhaps because nothing of what it implied conflicted with general linguistic theory as it stood in the 'fifties and 'sixties. One could go farther and say that far from conflicting with contemporary structural thinking, this aspect of traditional studies was compatible with it and even deferred to it. What I am alluding to is the fact that traditional contact studies took as their point of departure language conceived of as a totality, a unity. They had to do with standardized languages referable to an identifiable culturo-political reality, a formalized entity that was understood to be homogeneous, or as near so as made no matter. Thus for example Fraser Mackenzie in his vast thesis *Les relations de l'Angleterre et de la France d'après le vocabulaire* (Paris, 1939) recounted in cultural terms the history of contacts between two accepted and virtually immutable data, the French language and the English language, whose existence and nature were deemed to be self-evident and in no need of definition. Since this is the kind of monograph I wish to take down from its shelf and if possible press into service again by justifying it in a modern context it will be convenient to give the approach it represents a name. The prefix *macro-* is available to be used in the sense accepted by social scientists — as when the term macro-economics is applied to research

involving the economic resources of a country taken as a whole. It has
already been applied in some areas of language studies. Bearing in mind this
concept of totality, of the accredited standard language viewed in its
entirety, we may plausibly speak of traditional *macro-contact* or *macro-
interference* studies.

As lexicologists are well aware, the sudden change of attitude towards
contact phenomena which occurred early in the 'fifties was essentially a shift
from interlingual to bilingual research. One associates it with the publication of Uriel Weinreich's outstandingly successful *Languages in Contact*,[4] but
as his bibliography of six hundred items indicates, Weinreich himself did
not launch the scientific study of bilingualism or create the actual strategy
which it adopted from then on. What he did do through the overwhelming
success of *Languages in Contact* was to give authority to an approach and a
terminology already familiar among ethnologists and others investigating
minority languages in America. At this point the spotlight swung away
from macro-studies based on established, generally literary languages
—what at one time would have been labelled 'languages of culture' — to
focus upon the linguistic status of minority groups and their efforts to
integrate linguistically with the accepted major language of the environment in which they found themselves. Very frequently these minorities
were immigrant, ex-immigrant or ethnic groups. Macro-contact studies
became marginal and have remained so ever since.

Just now I used the word 'revolutionary'. It is in the nature of revolutions
to by-pass any moderate attempts at reform which may be going on at the
time, however constructive or well-intentioned these may be. There were
many such attempts in our field. In the immediate post-war years
lexicologists, aware of their diminished status in a structural world, had
every incentive to look around them for new analytical and descriptive
methods. During the early 'fifties I myself tried in a small way to move
macro-contact studies in the direction of theoretical linguistics by seeking to
identify what in the process of lexical borrowing was due to the external
pressure of cultural change, and what to conditions prevailing at a given
moment within the language upon which the foreign influence was being
exerted. The research which ensued was inspired to some extent by the

[4] Uriel Weinreich, *Languages in Contact. Findings and Problems.* Publications of the Linguistic
Circle of New York, No 1 (New York, 1953; subsequent reprints by Mouton, The Hague).

concept of 'economy' expounded by functionalists like Martinet, and also by some of Einar Haugen's early writings (but not, as it happened, by Weinreich). The resulting theoretical model was called *lexical ecology*, a figure drawn from the natural sciences in the way Gilliéron and the early linguistic geographers drew theirs from medicine and the earth sciences *(hypertrophie sémantique, stratigraphie linguistique, thérapeutique verbale)*. What I wanted to do was to test the hypothesis that in at least some areas of vocabulary provision of new lexemes from foreign sources was materially influenced by semantic insufficiency (or more accurately, *inefficiency*) in respect of the significatory resources of the receiving language itself, so that neologisms acquired in this way could be said to be *induced* from within as well as *imposed* from without. The assumption was that a certain body of loan-words could be found where one judged that an onomasiological or 'word-and-thing' interpretation was too far-fetched or plainly inadequate to explain why the neologism came into being. On my interpretation of the data this assumption proved to be correct. It was then a reasonable inference that these semantic groupings or (as it often appeared) assortment of individual items represented the innovations in which semantic structure had in some way intervened, and hence were the appropriate corpus for an 'ecological' analysis to work on.[5]

It needs to be made quite clear that this use of the term *ecology* had nothing to do with the present-day conservationist and interventionist sense of the word familiar to learned and lay because of the current vogue of environmental studies. In the pre-Sputnik era of the 1950s emphasis was not

---

[5] The research method used had three stages: firstly, to prepare what was in effect a commented etymological dictionary of a large body of loan-words which passed between two established standard languages over a considerable period of time, in this case French and Italian, giving a total of some three thousand words; secondly, to apply a traditional 'history through loan-words' analysis to each item, attempting to account for as many as possible of the borrowings by *word-and-thing* relationships; and thirdly, to analyse the remaining items of vocabulary with the notion of semantic structure in mind. The corpus of material with a historical commentary and some general inferences was published in Hope, *Lexical Borrowing in the Romance Languages* (Oxford: Blackwell, 1971). Among other data the investigation furnished statistics about individual semantic categories borrowed which could claim to be more authentic than previous ones on account of the size of the corpus used. The proportion of 'non-onomasiological' borrowings reached its highest point during the period when France was most strongly influenced by the Italian Renaissance (ie in the same cultural context as that chosen by Ullmann for his investigation of English); here the proportion was about 15 per cent. In periods of less intense inter-cultural contact the proportion of borrowed vocabulary potentially subject to structural semantic modification was of the order of 5–7½ per cent.

on conservation but on using resources as intensively as possible to aid post-war reconstruction. Ecology in the later, environmental sense also had its linguistic analogue, dating effectively from Einar Haugen's use of the term in the title of his book *The Ecology of Language*, which appeared in 1972 (though the concept and the usage really belong to the previous decade).[6] This wider connotation of assessing a community's linguistic needs and influencing the pattern of languages which serve it is of course the 'ecological' sense now accepted among linguists, and it is closely bound up with *language planning* (commonly shortened to 'LP'), a department of applied linguistics whose prosperity again owes much to Haugen's guiding hand. Practitioners of LP tend to use the word in this way even when bilingualism is one of the chief parameters the language planner has to take into consideration (which it often is, because the need for planning characteristically arises where there is a choice between competing linguistic media, or where the language *in situ* falls short in practical respects and needs to be supplemented from elsewhere).[7]

As it happened the new interest in bilingualism outflanked all projects for refining macro-contact analysis, whether they took structural principles as their starting point or not. Why the new outlook succeeded so dramatically is easy to understand. It had both positive and negative advantages to offer. In positive terms, it dealt with the present day and therefore was synchronic rather than historical ('historicism' was at that time a disparaging word, like 'conceptualism' or 'referentialism'). Dealing with bilinguals and their speech habits yielded empirical research data acceptable to scholars in other disciplines, especially social scientists. Moreover bilingualism quickly came to occupy a privileged position within the expanding domain of socio-

---

[6] Einar Haugen, *The Ecology of Language*. Essays edited by Anwar S. Dil (Stanford: Stanford UP, 1972).

[7] While this article was being prepared two publications appeared using *ecology* in senses relevant to the present discussion. A recent book by Albert Doppagne entitled *Pour une écologie de la langue française* (Brussels: Commission française de la Culture de l'Agglomération de Bruxelles, 1979) reports on the present position of *franglais* in the Belgian capital. It consists of a critical glossary of current Anglicisms with suggested native equivalents, plus a series of essays on familiar puristic lines, somewhat in the vein of Etiemble, but more constructive and less rhetorical. A recent very substantial reprint of essays on language contact in the Trends in Linguistics series has a concluding chapter by Mackey entitled 'Towards an Ecology of Language Contact' (W. F. Mackey and J. Ornstein, *Sociolinguistic Studies in Language Contact: Methods and Cases*, Trends in Linguistics (ed W. Winter), Studies and Monographs 6 (The Hague: Mouton, 1979)). The argument here is a little closer to our own, being a plea for a concerted effort to co-ordinate the linguistic and non-linguistic factors that enter into the description of bilingualism (see also note 16).

linguistics. The cultural ambit of bilingualism within the context of minority groups is one of social dynamism. Situations arise which correspond exactly to those met with in classic examples of sociolinguistic research, especially those which interpret linguistic variation on the synchronic plane in terms of a hierarchy, as representing points on a scale of prestige and desirability. Negative factors, too, were favourable. Windy notions about world-views and *Zeitgeister* were out of character in a branch of study which above all aspired to be operationally valid; they could be replaced by concepts of group and language loyalty, which though still abstractions were capable of being investigated in the field. A purely linguistic advantage accrued from the fact that bilingual research could operate without constantly looking over its shoulder at Saussure's definition of *langue* as a homogeneous system applying in equal measure to all the speech community. Lastly the new, contemporary, sociologically-orientated bilingual research had something democratic and down-to-earth about it that was well in accord with the mood of the 'fifties. Written sources with their clerkly detachment and taint of prescriptive authoritarianism took second place, and priority was given to the flesh-and-blood vernacular of minorities who were also apt to be under-privileged and therefore especially interesting to those whose linguistics had a dash of political fervour in it.

Bilingual studies are still an expanding universe. The volume of research they generate shows no sign of slackening. It is certainly true that the kind of research opportunities open to young scholars has changed a good deal in North America, where the new wave began. At the present time, one generation after Weinreich, many of the old closely-knit immigrant groups have been absorbed, particularly those who came from Europe, in spite of their having brought strongly held loyalties and sophisticated social traditions with them. Yet new situations have arisen even in North America owing to massive immigration into the United States and Canada during the post-war period. These too have often involved speakers of European languages (above all Italian and Spanish; the latter, of course, mainly from non-European territories). The last two decades, however, have seen unprecedented numbers of new Americans arriving from East Asian countries and adding fresh dimensions to the problem of linguistic integration by their presence. It goes without saying that in the world at large, with the pace of interaction between communities accelerating

constantly, further opportunities for studying bilingualism and pluri-
lingualism, including their function in situations of diglossia, are virtually
limitless.

In spite of all that has been said so far in this essay, it seems to me that now
is an ideal time to take up the cause of macro-contact studies once more, at
the end of the third decade since minority bilingualism made its successful
take-over bid, so to speak. To be exact, traditional historico-cultural studies
never entirely lost momentum during the intervening period. It is probably
true to say that the best work ever done on contact between literary or
standard languages has been published during the last fifteen years. 'Best' is
perhaps an invidious term to use; but one cannot deny that recent works are
more likely to present us with reliable data (helped, no doubt, by the
constant move forward of etymological research) and that they make a
serious attempt to dig more deeply than the usual anecdotal reviews of
'mots voyageurs' which our 'témoins de l'histoire' are apt to do — an
attempt, that is, to reform in their own way the abuses that Professor
Oksaar and the bilingual theorists were rebelling against during the 'sixties.[8]

But the reasons why a reappraisal is due bear little relation to work done
in the *genre* itself. They have to do with changes brought about by time,
which brings in his revenges in linguistics as in everything else. Although
these shifts of perspective are historical by nature they have two quite
different points of focus: firstly, there are changes in the climate of linguistic
research, leading to new ideas about what in the discipline is admissible, and
what peripheral or inappropriate; and secondly, changes in the political
status of standard languages (or 'cultural languages', or *langues de grande
diffusion*) as seen in their relation to the contemporary world.

Both these points call for amplification.

Those who did not have to live through the age of high structuralism, of
strictly formal descriptive linguistics, will find it hard to appreciate how

[8] Cf with reference to the Romance languages: G. L. Beccaria, *Spagnolo e spagnoli in Italia.
Riflessi ispanici sulla lingua italiana del Cinque e del Seicento* (Turin: Giappichelli, 1968); T. E.
Hope, *op cit*, 1971; I. Klajn, *Influssi inglesi nella lingua italiana*, Accademia Toscana di Scienze e
Lettere 'La Colombaria', Studi 22 (Florence: Olschki, 1972); A. Goldiş-Poalelungi,
L'influence du français sur le roumain (vocabulaire et syntaxe), Publications de l'Université de
Dijon No 64 (Paris: Belles lettres, 1973); K. Gebhardt, *Das okzitanische Lehngut im
Französischen*, Heidelberger Beiträge zur Romanistik Bd 3 (Bern-Frankfurt: Lang, 1974).

restrictive the prevailing attitude was towards a good deal of the work which went on under the heading of semantics, and more particularly the two specialisms that most people referred to as historical semantics and lexicology. Some technical terms became taboo, among them *content*. Although fundamental to vocabulary studies the notion of content was repugnant to most linguists because it was felt to imply that concepts could exist divorced from the formal expression which alone rendered them accessible to the senses and so brought them within the scope of a behaviouristic, mechanistic analysis. An earnest of the way the tide is setting in favour of lexical linguists nowadays may be found in the way Bendix's componential semantics has become accepted, even to the extent of its being considered a legitimate basis on which to build models for a semantic component of transformational-generative grammar. I myself cannot easily forget that when at a learned gathering in Newcastle nearly twenty years ago the late Danish scholar Jens Holt read a paper about the interpretation of *figurae of content* as laid down in the glossematists' canon he provoked a reaction very near to ridicule. His audience pointed out that replacing a single morpheme, *man*, by three others, *human*, *male* and *adult*, was merely elaboration and nothing resembling analysis at all. Yet the thesis on which Holt's *Pleremics* rested, and for that matter its practical realization, corresponded almost exactly to the 'componential' model proposed by Bendix a decade later and accepted since then by Bierwisch, Lyons, Katz, Postal, Fodor — and indeed by virtually all contemporary semanticists.

The same anti-mentalistic fervour brought about a curiously ambivalent attitude towards another stand-by of lexical analysis, field theory. Seductive because it offered a hope of delineating the major areas of lexis in structural terms, it was nevertheless highly suspect on account of its blatant 'referentialism' and the close links with content analysis which were part and parcel of its methodology.

There is no need by now to labour the truism that Chomsky's transformational grammar also rested on frankly mentalistic premises. 'Deep structure' comes as near as anyone could wish to a 'collection of disembodied meanings', to those 'ideas without their verbal clothing' that descriptive linguists refused to have any truck with.[9]

[9] Cf W. Haas, 'The Theory of Translation', *Philosophy* 37 (1962), esp p 210.

Semantics, of course, is itself an equivocal term which can bear many different interpretations, as Ullmann himself knew perfectly well. At the opposite pole from his own referentially based, onomasiological-historical approach (which was also approved by a near-totality of European semanticists from Bréal and Gombocz to Kronasser and Gamillscheg) lay the austere scepticism of Harris, Trager and the other Bloomfieldians; separate again, but more broadly based and more enterprising intellectually came Firth and his followers, representing the maximal interest in semantics shown by any linguistic school. Firth's *spectrum of meaning* had a place for lexical semantics among the 'major functions' of meaning, a postulate traditional European interlinguists would have felt comfortable with if they had taken the trouble to see what the London school had to offer.[10] His interpretation of context of situation, though a little ragged at the edges, was also something that promised well from the lexicologist's point of view. Since Firth's day the original root-stock of semantic theory has produced an efflorescence of new blooms and not a few sports in the fields of semiology, pragmatics and semiotics.[11] But my object in ranging over some of the options available is not to praise times past or fight old battles again. What I want to do is to point out as forcibly as possible that for a whole gamut of reasons the attitude of theoretical linguists towards certain concepts which need to be put to use in interlinguistic research has become infinitely more liberal during the last decade, and that because of this any branch of study based on lexis can now be considered admissible as a scholarly pursuit as far as the majority of colleagues are concerned.

To return to the position of cultural languages. Even in this more favourable climate of opinion we may still ask, I take it, whether the study of macro-interference as we have just defined it has anything to propose which is not already allowed for under the 'minority bilingual' or

[10] The relevant passage runs as follows: 'Meaning . . . we use for the whole complex of functions which a linguistic form may have. The principal components of this whole meaning are phonetic function, which I call a minor function, the major functions — lexical, morphological and syntactical — and the function of a complete locution in the context of situation' ('The Technique of Semantics', *Trans Philol Soc* (1935), p 72).

[11] Literary semiologists like Barthes and the *Tel Quel* group as well as practical or scientific semiologists like Buyssens and Mounin all make a point of insisting on their debt to Saussure's *science qui étudie la vie des signes au sein de la vie sociale*. Many lines of thought which are primarily extra-linguistic like ethnomethodology or cognitive sociology as expounded by Cicourel have a good deal to say about understanding meaning as a pre-requisite to defining social interaction — an insight Firth would have recognized and approved of.

'socio-dynamic' heading. Presumably there is at least one reason for studying standard languages in an interlinguistic setting, and that is — to use the current idiom — simply the fact that the opportunity is there. There exists an identifiable domain which is being neglected at present by serious linguists, and ought not to be. Standard languages are generally literary languages as well; we might wish to be informed, for example, about the nature of contact phenomena whose motivation is stylistic in the sense that they possess what Ullmann, with acknowledgements to Charles Bally, called *evocative values*.[12] But practical promptings to undertake research in this alternative area, compelling though they may be, are less important than considerations of principle. Why macro-contact studies deserve a new look is because they have become operationally valid. In the present socio-political climate they are relevant for reasons that remind one of the way in which bilingual studies, for their part, became relevant during the 'fifties. For the fact is that bilingual studies too started because the problem was there. We have seen already how they developed *pari passu* with increasing self-awareness on the part of plurilingual communities. Thirty years ago sociological and linguistic sensibilities coincided to produce an interlinguistics worthy of the times, which was that of Weinreich and his followers. At the present moment a similar meeting of viewpoints is preparing to usher in new methods. They are methods which in certain respects square neatly with the traditional or 'old-fashioned' modes of thought. They also — be it said in passing — chime in with the culturally oriented and socially stratified points of view which were familiar to Ullmann as a young scholar and which led him in the early works we have mentioned to realize his interlingual research in terms of the chief standard languages of Europe.

In the past thirty years the great majority of communities large and small throughout the world have become increasingly group-conscious, politically organized and nationalistic. For the most part they have proved to be

---

[12] A mutual interest in this aspect of contact phenomena helped to cement the lasting friendship between Ullmann and W. Theodor Elwert, who more than anyone has been responsible for investigating the stylistic value of foreign linguistic resources in the Romance field. It is worth while noting that when Ullmann moved towards stylistic studies in the early 'fifties his research into loan-words used by individual authors provided him with a bridge. From 1949 to 1951 he wrote several articles on the stylistic role of Anglicisms in French Romantic authors, and these with the addition of similar studies on Italianisms and Hispanisms provided the basis of the initial chapter of his first monograph on style ('Some Romantic experiments in local colour', *Style in the French Novel* (Cambridge: CUP, 1957), pp 40–93).

interventionists in their attitude to the new problems that went hand in hand with this new awareness, and directivists as regards the practical steps they have chosen to take to resolve them. As always, language tends to reflect the vagaries of the culture it serves, so we may expect to find some of these characteristics carried over into the use of language and the speech community's attitude towards it. There is an artificiality, a self-awareness in the functioning of language at the present day that was not evident in the past, or at any rate not evident to anything like the same degree. Language planning is one aspect of this new directivism. There are other pieces of evidence which point in the same direction, less conspicuous perhaps, but significant. The decline in dialectology and corresponding rise in socio-linguistics is a case in point; the shift, that is, from dialect studies based on a time-honoured, 'natural' conception of language variety corresponding to territorial extension, towards the far more complex urban dialects, structured and explicable in terms of class, wealth and other socio-economic parameters to which the linguistic patterns may serve as a pointer.[13] A minority-based, socially dynamic type of bilingual study may also be said to be 'natural' or normal in certain respects. The principle which gives this kind of interaction its impetus is one of choice leading to continuous progress towards better things, including a steady advance upwards through the various layers of accepted society; the whole paralleled in the gradual mutations to which a bilingual's speech is subject. I have no doubt that Weinreich and other interlinguists of his day had this conception at the back of their minds. But here again this picture seems less clearly contoured to contemporary eyes. An effort of the imagination is needed nowadays to envisage life as an open-ended opportunity to pursue one's individual inclinations, as a steady working out of natural urges for personal betterment. At best these ideals now appear to be endemic only in certain areas, and though widespread they are not universal. In other places, and certainly at other times, the reality of the human condition was not conceived of in such terms as these.

---

[13] Other scientists see themselves denied the comfort of long-accepted, 'natural' norms in a similar way and find that they too have to make a niche in their methodology for what is willed, contrived, subject to human inclination. Ornithologists and zoologists, for instance, who find that they have to bring oil pollution or diseases such as myxomatosis into their calculations. The radical shift of interest from anthropology to sociology which also occurred during the 'fifties and 'sixties is closely analogous to that we have just drawn attention to from dialectology to sociolinguistics.

I do not want to press the 'natural versus artificial' argument for more than it is worth, and in any case I am conscious of the well-known risk of over-simplifying. Even Weinreich (who after all learned his interlinguistics from the same tradition as Ullmann) was aware of the useful part to be played by *macro*-studies and historico-cultural reconstruction; so much so that he saw his own techniques as an auxiliary to older methods, as well as an improvement on them. 'It has long been customary' he observed in *Languages in Contact* (pp 109–10) 'to use the evidence of cultural loanwords to reconstruct social, cultural and political conditions under which the borrowings were made. If the study of actual cases of language contact should show that certain types of interference are habitualized under specific socio-cultural conditions, but not under others, then it may be possible to buttress the reconstruction of social situations of the past with the help of linguistic evidence other than cultural loanwords alone.' And a glance at W. F. Mackey's monumental *Bibliographie internationale sur le bilinguisme* (Quebec, 1972), which at the time of publication a decade ago listed no fewer than ten thousand items, shows how remarkably the bilingual approach has diversified, to the extent that it has overlapped with the older type of monograph in certain spheres.

Perhaps what I am advocating is a change of emphasis rather than one of direction, but all things considered I do not think the situation facing interlinguistics can be so easily rationalized as that. All ways of looking at either bilingualism in the more austere sense or interference in a wider frame of reference have a great deal in common. Bilingual speakers always play a part somewhere, whether one thinks of Cuban soldiers adapting their L_1 to make contact with Portuguese-based native speakers in Angola or a young European fanatic of popular music speaking an in-language anchored firmly in American teenage usage. But the difference of degree, if it is one, has to cover extremely divergent cases. What one actually sees happening on the ground at the present time is nothing like so simple as the bilingual doctrine seems to imply. We have before us examples of languages being prescribed in specific forms rather than others according to directives issued by educators; state-financed purism supported by appeals to the national interest through the mass media, or frankly imposed by law; constraints applied to the normal wastage of small language communities, as when minor languages like Rhaeto-Romance are fostered for cultural and folkloristic ends. We see people owing allegiance to a hierarchy of linguistic empires and taking up a notably different stance towards each level — a Welshman, for example, who is bilingual in Welsh and English, or native Catalan and Breton speakers who currently use Spanish and French. In some of these instances the circumstance of bilingualism remains an important factor; but in very many bilingualism as such, and *a fortiori* the analysis of an individual bilingual's speech habits, have become mere incidentals, with no strong bid to make for a researcher's time. Where did bilingualism enter into the pattern when, say, a pre-war Italian government committee decided first to tax the use of the word *bar*, then reluctantly revised their decision because it was semantically indispensable? It would not be impossible to think up a bilingual scenario. One could imagine an Italian repatriate, wealthy as well as Anglophone after a lifetime's work in New York, returning to his native province and setting up a chain of hotels each with its lucrative *bar americano*. But a researcher who was only curious to know what the Bowery had contributed to the phonemic/allophonic pattern of the great hotelier's native Milanese would be missing a good deal of the vast configuration of activity — linguistic, sociolinguistic and extralinguistic — to which Mussolini's LP treatment of the loan-word *bar* was a valuable clue.

In putting forward this tentative plea that one should cultivate a sort of informed revisionism towards existing methods with a view to bringing interlinguistic studies up to date I have spent most of my time talking about changes in climates of opinion inside and outside the accepted linguistic field. I have tried to exemplify these by tracing a changing attitude to semantics and hinting at what seems to me to be a significant shift in social and political awareness during the recent past. There is however a lot more to be said than this. Arguments which might be adduced in favour of a fresh approach to *macro*-contact studies do not all rest on abstractions, are not all based on the opportunities offered by theoretical background and changing attitudes. A new deal would also be timely on practical and empirical grounds.

When Ullmann set out to show what Europe owed to the English language he was thinking exclusively of British English and of the part it played during the eighteenth and nineteenth centuries, the formative period of modern European civilization. At that time the contribution of American English was not material to the main cultural drift. Even when Ullmann was writing, the word *franglais* (or *spanglish*, or *sovjangliski* or any other portmanteau with the same interlingual goods inside), had not yet been coined, and the linguistic upheavals which such terms connote were still undreamt of. Today, as everyone knows, the impact of American English on the world is a sociolinguistic fact of unrivalled importance. By its very existence it is enough to put a *macro-* approach back on the agenda, as Firth would say. It is a challenging objective reality, a fascinating sector of the real world of language, part of the wood we so often find hard to see for gazing too intently at theoretical trees. Other examples of conflict and adjustment between politically and culturally accredited standards will crop up in the future, and probably with increasing frequency as the trend towards interaction gathers momentum (which one assumes it will, failing some global catastrophe which sets human beings back at arm's length from each other again). But for the next few years Anglo-American influences on the languages of Western Europe will continue to be available as a ready-made proving ground where we hope to find the answer to some of the questions interlinguists have asked since last century. What actually occurs when — as we put it, figuratively — established languages come into conflict as a result of political or cultural contact? What kind and degree of influence is exerted by language loyalty and by purism? What, indeed, do these unsatisfactory lexical superordinates mean? What part is played by the media, press agencies, publicity, technical co-operation and rivalry? How can we account for negative factors such as inertia, time-lag, historical accident or even sheer chance, if such a thing can be deemed to exist in the analytical disciplines? Is it at all a practical proposition to construct a sort of calculus which would relate in a meaningful way such disparate interference factors as the semantic structure of a borrowing language, political unification, interventionist ideologies, prejudice and liberalism, self-expression and aesthetic creativity?

   One fact that stands out clearly from this diverse prospectus is the importance of *lexis*. It is true that research work already completed indicates that Americanism during the last thirty years has made an impact on European languages at all levels, and that syntactical borrowings or calques of idioms and clichés afford very distinctive insights into the nature of cultural influences, quite apart from their value as exponents to measure the degree of influence by. But lexicalization is still of prime importance for the perfectly straightforward reason that lexicalized items correspond (in a way which we have not yet fully grasped, though we sense its importance) to a crystallizing of interest upon certain cultural features on the part of a given language community.[14]

Conceding pride of place to lexemic contact has, however, an important sequel in that it brings us back to the inherent problem of lexis which has lain before each school of linguistic thought in succession without ever being tackled effectively (least of all by descriptive structuralism). The problem is of course the old one of Language and Life; and though we may find the Jespersenian conception naïve we still cannot justify our condescension by claiming that we have solved it in any convincing manner — or even fully understood what it implies. 'It is accepted', observes Lyons, 'that a particular language will reflect in its vocabulary the culture of the society for which it is the medium of expression.'[15] The principle is basic, and as an abstract concept, certainly, it is universally received among lexicologists. But how this proposition can be proved to have the validity we spontaneously accord to it is so daunting a prospect that few people have ever faced up to it. Those who have, like Matoré, are inclined to subordinate lexis to sociology — a fact which does not demote the lexicologist from his functions (any more than Chomsky's views about language and psychology eliminate the linguist), but merely assumes that he should be willing to co-operate across disciplines with the social scientists. Such a possibility upsets us less nowadays, when the linguist's battle for autonomy is a thing of the past and one can well afford not only to look outwards again but actively to seek advice and help from the fields of study surrounding core linguistics. The interlinguist's (and the lexicologist's) underlying ambition must be to state as fully and as scientifically as possible the constraints which bear upon the equation *language* = *life*. We

[14] Cf G. Matoré, *La méthode en lexicologie* (Paris: Didier, 1953), p 36. A great deal of work still remains to be done on the status of lexis in interference studies, despite the fact that so many articles and monographs have been written on this aspect of contact. It is obvious that there is as much variation in the role of the many different items subsumed under the title of lexis as there is between borrowing at the lexical level and, say, syntactic calque. If we aspire to incorporate semantic structure into our description, for instance, we shall do well to take into account the slots occupied by different analytical levels of lexicalization from superordinate down to subordinate via perhaps a number of intermediate componential groupings, including what Lakoff refers to as 'maximal clusters of humanly-related properties' (cf *Papers from the Fifteenth Regional Meeting, Chicago Linguistic Society*, 1979, esp pp 243–4). One's impression is that borrowed superordinates are quite common (cf Hope, *Lexical Borrowing*, pp 727–9). The motives underlying such borrowings offer interesting ground for speculation, whether one seeks to explain them linguistically or culturally.

[15] J. Lyons, *Structural Semantics*, Publ Philol Soc 20 (Oxford: Blackwell, 1963), pp 40–1.

have to put together as many as possible of the kind of conditioning factors listed just now and try to assess their relative weight and the extent to which they interact in a given, real environment. The enterprise may seem a hopelessly intractable attempt to equate unlike terms; but this is partly because we have fallen into the habit of disregarding Wittgenstein's good advice by theorizing first and looking afterwards. We are not required to set up an interlocking pattern of constraints *a priori*. The immediate task is to *comprehend* in all senses of the term the actual situation on the ground presented by American English and the Western European languages. We need to put language back into its context — *replacer le langage dans son milieu*, as Robert-Léon Wagner and his pupils wisely insisted[16] — and make ourselves as informed as possible about what exactly is happening both inside and outside language when large-scale confrontation takes place between standard languages of high prestige in the interactive world of today.

One might ask why a linguist should do these things. Perhaps he should not. Perhaps what we need to look for is a different kind of researcher, someone who is part linguist, part something else, and give him a new discipline to identify himself by. Or perhaps we need to take linguistics in hand and alter that. At least there is no doubt that both international contact and its interlinguistic *éminence grise* exist and produce effects which can be observed. It is also true that these interlinguistic factors are at this very

---

[16] Cf K. J. Hollyman, *Le développement du vocabulaire féodal en France pendant le haut moyen âge* (Geneva: Droz, 1957), p 2. Of the references quoted the one to Sir Alan Gardiner is much the most specific statement made at that time, when the relationship between language and culture (or language and anthropology) was accepted as a proper topic for the 'philologist' to devote himself to. Gardiner spoke of the need to put back acts of speech 'into their original setting of real life, and thence to discover what processes are employed, what factors involved' (*The Theory of Speech and Language* (Oxford: Clarendon Press, 1932), p 6). One oberves with interest that Malinowski's work on the language of the Trobriand Islanders, which Hollyman also mentions, had a profound influence on those aspects of J. R. Firth's linguistic thinking to which reference has already been made.
I note in passing that the 'uncommitted' approach suggested here differs materially from that which Mackey puts forward in his 'ecological' chapter cited earlier (note 7). Though Mackey is eclectic in his choice of indices and sampling techniques his purpose in the long run is to define bilingualism more efficaciously — ie to follow up the celebrated work he has already done on the measurement of bilingualism by mathematical procedures. In other words he proposes to stay firmly within the ambit of linguistics. I do not of course suggest that this mode of research is not valuable; only that it is not unique. In any case the linguist's particular expertise is indispensable even when an investigation embraces peripheral areas. Contact studies, one might argue, are a matter for linguists, but not exclusively a linguistic matter.

F

moment playing an active role in the changes which, whether we call them evolution, progress or continuous revolution, are going to count for something important as far as the future human condition is concerned. Would it be too ambitious to suggest that *macro*-contact studies pursued with the help of resources commensurate with the research and the problems involved, might end by bringing suggestive new facts to light about social interaction and social change?

Somehow I think that Ullmann, while gently criticizing both the style and the brashness of such a rhetorical question, would have been prepared to sit down and write you out a bibliography that would have gone at least half way towards answering it.

Structural Semantics in Retrospect

JOHN LYONS

Professor of Linguistics, University of Sussex

1. Introduction

In the years that have passed since the publication of my book, *Structural Semantics* (1963), I have often been asked to produce for the benefit of those who do not know Classical Greek a synopsis, in English, of the analysis of the vocabulary of Plato that was presented, without translation or glosses, in Part 2 of that work.[1] It is my intention, in this article, to provide such a synopsis and, in doing so, to relate the results of the analysis to one of the present-day concerns in lexical semantics: the notion of focal meaning and semantic prototypes.

It is highly appropriate that, this article being written, it should appear in the present volume. Twenty-five years ago I first read Stephen Ullmann's *Principles of Semantics* (1951) and in consequence became, almost overnight, a structural semanticist. I had already decided that my PhD research would be on the vocabulary of Plato. Ullmann's account of the theory of lexical fields (Wortfelder), and more especially of Jost Trier's famous analysis of the Middle High German field of words relating to knowledge and understanding, confirmed my decision and opened my eyes to the fact that the vocabularies of different languages are not necessarily isomorphic. When I eventually produced my PhD dissertation (of which *Structural Semantics*, published three years later, was a slightly revised version), Ullmann himself was one of the examiners. There is a sense, therefore, in which he was, without having been directly involved with it during the years of its writing, one of its prime movers and one of its final arbiters. As one of the principal exponents of post-Saussurean structuralism writing in English and 'einer der massgeblichen Begründer des "renouveau de la

---

[1] J. Lyons, *Structural Semantics: An Analysis of Part of the Vocabulary of Plato*. Publications of the Philological Society, 20 (Oxford: Blackwell, 1963).

sémantique"' that took place in the 1950s,[2] he would have approved, I am sure, of what I am attempting here. I therefore dedicate my article to his memory, in gratitude for all that he taught me through his writings and for the kindness that he showed me in more recent years when I came to know him personally.

2. Theoretical and methodological considerations

I will here set out, with minimal explanation and discussion, some of the principles upon which the analysis rests. Many of these are definitive of the particular, somewhat eclectic, version of structuralism to which I was, and except for differences of detail or emphasis still am, committed. In reformulating them here, I will make use, as far as possible, of the terminology and notational conventions introduced in my book *Semantics*, published in 1977.[3]

(i)   Every language has, to a greater or lesser degree, its own unique grammatical and lexical structure. It is for this reason that word-for-word translation between any two natural languages is, in general, impossible. Point (i) is relatively uncontroversial.

(ii)   As far as natural languages are concerned, the related principles of expressibility, effability and universality, as expounded by such authors as Hjelmslev, Tarski, Searle, and Katz, are of doubtful validity, if not definitely fallacious.[4] It should not therefore be taken for granted that languages are intertranslatable at the level of sentences, statements or propositions. It is for this reason that I did not provide English glosses for any of the Greek in Part 2 of *Structural Semantics*. (I return to this point below, in connection with my present attempt to explain to those who do

[2] Cf H. Geckeler, *Strukturelle Bedeutungslehre* (Darmstadt: Wissenschaftliche Buchgesellschaft, 1978), p 3.

[3] J. Lyons, *Semantics*, 2 vols (Cambridge: Cambridge UP, 1977).

[4] L. Hjelmslev, *Omkring Sprogteoriens Grundlaeggelse* (Copenhagen, 1943); English translation by F. J. Whitfield, *Prolegomena to a Theory of Language* (Bloomington, Ind: Indiana UP, 1953), p 97. A. Tarski, 'The Semantical Conception of Truth', *Philosophy and Phenomenological Research*, 4 (1944), pp 341–75. (Reprinted in Tarski, *Logic, Semantics, Metamathematics*, London: Oxford UP, 1956). J. R. Searle, *Speech Acts* (London: Cambridge UP, 1969), pp 19 ff. J. J. Katz, *Semantic Theory* (New York: Harper and Row, 1972), pp 19 ff.

not know Greek at least something of the meaning of certain Platonic words
and expressions. It should be noted that the fact that one can, with more or less
success and by means of successive approximation, explain in metalanguage
L_X what is meant by some expression of the object language L_Y does not imply
that the L_Y expression is translatable into L_X. There is some confusion on this
point in discussions of expressibility and universality.) Point (ii) does not
follow from point (i) and would be rejected by many structuralists.

(iii)   To speak a language is to engage in a particular kind of social activity,
which is regulated in part by culturally variable norms. Furthermore, the
language-system itself, and in particular the vocabulary, is structured, to a
significant degree, by culture-dependent distinctions; it is part of what
Wittgenstein in his *Philosophical Investigations* called a form of life. This does
not imply that there are no culture-independent, and perhaps biologically
determined, semantic distinctions.[5] Nor does it imply, as proponents of the
more extreme versions of Humboldtian or Whorfian relativism have maintained, that it is impossible to acquire a more or less adequate degree of
competence in the production and understanding of utterances and texts in
languages other than one's own native language. But it does imply that one's
degree of competence in another language is limited by one's assimilation of
the culture-dependent social norms and semantic distinctions associated with
the language in question.

Clearly, the semantic analysis of texts in a dead language poses more serious
methodological problems, from this point of view, than does the semantic
analysis of texts in a living language for which informants are available and in
the use of which the investigator can himself operate as a participant-observer
in a wide range of relevant situations. However, it is my assumption (for which
some justification is offered in *Structural Semantics*) that traditional classical
scholarship provides us with a sufficiently accurate and detailed account of the
relevant aspects of Greek culture of the period for the analysis to proceed. I will
not go further into this question here.

The Platonic corpus, consisting of some two thousand pages of text, is
particularly good, by virtue of both its form and its content, for the semantic
analysis of the words that I was interested in. But the results of any purely
corpus-based analysis of the vocabulary of a language, however large the

[5] Cf Lyons, *Semantics*, p 248.

corpus of material, are bound to be incomplete and in certain respects speculative.

(iv)   Several of the lexemes that fall within the scope of the analysis are key-words in the sense of Williams,[6] and also in the roughly comparable sense of Matoré.[7] Furthermore, they are words that play an important part in the formulation of Plato's own epistemological and ontological theories.

As a matter of methodological principle, I have taken the view that Plato's philosophical use of the words is grounded in, but does not bear direct witness to, their normal meaning in the society of which he was a member; and I have taken the same view in respect of explicit definitions that are put forward for discussion (and usually rejected) in the dialogues.

This would be the attitude that I would adopt (though obviously there are additional methodological controls that can be introduced) if I were carrying out a corpus-based analysis of the English words 'knowledge', 'belief', 'understanding', etc, and using as part of my corpus philosophical or non-philosophical discussions either of knowledge or of 'knowledge' (in so far as the two kinds of discussions can be distinguished). For example, confronted with the assertion by someone using English that 'knowledge' means "justified true belief" (or alternatively — if indeed this is a genuine alternative — that knowledge is justified true belief) I would, as a matter of principle, distrust the factual content of the definition itself, but take it as an indication that 'knowledge' might prove to have a close semantic relation to 'belief' and also to 'truth' in the structure of the vocabulary of everyday English. It might turn out, of course, that the philosophically important relation between 'knowledge' and 'belief', though grounded in the everyday use of these words (and of the corresponding verbs 'know' and 'believe') is but one of several equally important relations which determine their sense. It so happens that, although I did start the analysis by including in it the Greek word 'doxa', which is usually translated in philosophical contexts as either 'belief' or 'opinion', I did not systematically pursue this line of investigation. I may well do so on some future occasion. I would emphasize that the analysis makes no claim to being complete: see point (vii) below.

[6] R. Williams, *Keywords: A Vocabulary of Culture and Society* (London: Fontana, 1976), p 13.
[7] G. Matoré, *La Méthode en lexicologie* (Paris: Didier, 1953), p 68. Cf S. Ullmann, *Semantics: An Introduction to the Science of Meaning* (Oxford: Blackwell, 1962), pp 252–3.

(v)   Semantic analysis does not require, in practice or in theory, a special metalinguistic vocabulary of universal semantic components.[8] The sense-relations that hold within a lexical field can be stated in terms of what Carnap (1952) called meaning postulates applying directly to the words of the object-language.[9] (This point is now more widely accepted by linguists than it was a few years ago.) In the following section I will make use of a modified and slightly extended version of English as my metalanguage. The fact that, for the present purpose, I need to use English, not only to talk about Greek, but also to talk about what Greek was used to talk about, creates particular problems. We cannot reasonably assume that words like 'knowledge', 'understanding' or 'skill' denote independently-existent and culturally-universal entities in the way that the names of animals, plants or physical artefacts do. Nor can we assume, as Trier and many other structuralists (including perhaps Saussure) have done, that there is a common conceptual content-substance divided up differently by different languages, such that the English word 'knowledge' and the Greek word 'episteme' (which is the nearest translational equivalent in most contexts) are correlated with more or less the same conceptual area.[10]

For present purposes, I will use English words to talk about Greek institutions and practices, whenever one can do so without distortion or misrepresentation of the point at issue. For example, I would use 'doctor' and 'medicine' to refer to what one would refer to in Greek by means of the words 'iatros' and 'iatrike', respectively. (As will be evident to those who know Greek, I am making use of a simplified system of trans-literation, which dispenses with accents, distinctions of vowel-length and the indication of a so-called smooth breathing.) The inter-language equivalence of 'doctor' and 'iatros' in so far as they are equivalent, can be justified, in principle, in terms of our ability to use the words correctly, once we have come to acquire an understanding of the society and culture in which they operate. It can also be justified, in the present instance, in terms of what Quine has called the continuum of cultural development.[11]

[8] Cf Lyons, *Semantics*, pp 317 ff.
[9] R. Carnap, 'Meaning Postulates', *Philosophical Studies*, 3 (1952), pp 65–73. (Reprinted in *Meaning and Necessity*, 2nd edn, Chicago: Univ of Chicago Press, 1956).
[10] Cf Lyons, *ibid*, p 260.
[11] W. V. O. Quine, *Word and Object* (Cambridge, Mass: MIT Press, 1960), p 76.

When it would be misleading to use English words to talk about what Plato and other members of the society to which he belonged used Greek to talk about, I will augment the vocabulary of English by making use of one of two techniques. The first consists in borrowing from Greek the citation-form of the appropriate word, duly transliterated, and treating it as the base-form of a word of English. For example, making use of this technique, I will treat 'episteme', 'tekhne' and 'sophia' from a syntactic and morphological point of view as if they were English words and semantically as if they were Greek. The second technique consists in modifying the form of a roughly equivalent English word by means of a mnemonic prefix. For example, I will use the noun 'T-knowledge' and the verb 'T-know' to refer to particular kinds of what, using English, I must call knowledge, but which in Greek falls within the scope of a more specific term. It will emerge from the analysis that 'tekhne' and 'T-knowledge' are in fact synonymous.

There is of course no sharp cut-off point between translationally equivalent and translationally non-equivalent expressions. The technique of extending the vocabulary of English by borrowing from Greek, in either of the two ways just outlined, results in a rather unidiomatic style of writing and will be used sparingly. However, it has the advantage of continually reminding the reader of what is actually being done when one language is being employed as a metalanguage with respect to another.

(vi) The sense of a lexically complex expression is a compositional function of the sense of its constituent lexemes: this is by now a widely accepted view.

The analysis reported in *Structural Semantics* was, as far as I am aware, the first in which the compositionality of the sense of complex expressions was explicated, in principle and in practice, within the framework of Chomskyan generative grammar. Since the late 1950s, when the analysis was carried out, there have been many semantically relevant modifications made by Chomksy and his successors to the theory of generative grammar.[12] None of these modifications would have had any effect upon the results of the analysis that was reported in *Structural Semantics*, though

[12] Cf J. D. Fodor, *Semantics: Theories of Meaning in Generative Grammar* (New York: Crowell, 1977).

they might well have influenced their formulation and presentation. At most, I should have been obliged, if I had been carrying out the analysis some ten years later than I did, to take into account the still unresolved controversy with respect to the lexicalist and transformationalist treatment of derivational morphology.[13]

In what follows, I adopt a rather traditional view of what constitutes a lexeme. However, I make use of nominalizing and adjectivalizing trans- formations as a means of relating lexemes to one another, syntagmatically and paradigmatically, within what is pre-theoretically identifiable as the field of knowledge and understanding, as this is structured in Platonic Greek. It is my belief that, whether transformational rules are strictly necessary or not as far as the generative capacity of a grammar is concerned, nominalizing and adjectivalizing transformations of the kind to which I appeal provide the semanticist with an elegant and perspicuous way of displaying the regularities by virtue of which the user of the language- system can draw inferences between statements containing syntagmatically and paradigmatically related lexemes and, as we shall see, can, in certain circumstances, create new lexemes whose meaning will be understood by others. Unlike Katz and Fodor[14] and their successors, I am concerned primarily with lexical semantics and only incidentally with sentence semantics; and I do not assume that it is the task of the semantic description of a language-system to assign to each of the syntactically and morpho- logically well-formed sentences generated by the grammar one or more semantic representations.[15]

(vii)   The analysis that was reported in *Structural Semantics* was necessarily incomplete; and what will be presented below is but a part of it. The reader must not think that I am attempting to provide a complete account of the meaning of the Greek words that I shall cite. Actually, I doubt whether there is any sense in which the analysis of the meaning of a word could ever claim to be complete, since I incline to the view that, apart from technical

---

[13] Cf N. Chomsky, 'Remarks on nominalization', in R. A. Jacobs and P. S. Rosenbaum (eds), *Readings in English Transformational Grammar* (Waltham, Mass: Ginn, 1970). (Reprinted in Chomsky, *Studies in Semantics and Generative Grammar* (The Hague: Mouton, 1972).

[14] J. J. Katz and J. A. Fodor, 'The Structure of a Semantic Theory', *Language*, 39 (1963), pp 170–210.

[15] Cf Lyons, *Semantics*, pp 409 ff.

terms whose sense is controlled by stipulative definition, words in natural languages do not have a fully determinate meaning. However that may be, in the following sections I want to make statements at the same level of generality as those which Ullmann made in his summary of Trier's analysis of the Middle High German vocabulary.[16] The inevitable consequence is that I shall be obliged to omit a lot of qualifying detail and shall tend to give the impression that the structure of the lexical field with which I am concerned is more systematic and neater than, in fact, it is. For the necessary qualifications I must refer the interested reader to *Structural Semantics*.

(viii)   Conventional dictionary definitions are not to be trusted. Particular dictionaries may be more or less adequate to the purpose for which they are compiled. All too often, however, the traditional procedure of starting a lexical entry with either the earliest attested or the most general sense of a word leads to misrepresentation of the way the word functions in the everyday language. Bilingual dictionaries tend to suffer from the additional distorting influence of translation: cf points (ii) and (iii) above. As far as the standard Greek-English dictionary is concerned (Liddell and Scott),[17] it is widely acknowledged to be, in various respects, unsystematic and unreliable. The inadequacy, and at times the incorrectness, of its definitions and glosses in lexical entries for the field of knowledge and understanding is readily demonstrated.

But the actual inadequacy of existing dictionaries is one thing; the theoretical inadequacy of all dictionary definitions, if they are construed as statements of meaning, is another. It is now more generally accepted by linguists and psychologists, and perhaps also by an increasing number of philosophers of language, than it was when *Structural Semantics* was written that for most words in the everyday, non-technical vocabulary of a language it is impossible, not only in practice, but also in principle, to formulate necessary and sufficient conditions determining their extension. Speakers of a language seem to operate with quite particularized, proto-typical, or focal, meanings, making contextual adjustments to these

---

[16] *The Principles of Semantics*, Glasgow Univ Publications, 84 (Glasgow: Jackson, 1951), pp 165 ff; also *Semantics: An Introduction to the Science of Meaning*, pp 248 ff.

[17] H. G. Liddell and R. Scott, *A Greek-English Lexicon*, 9th edition. Revised and augmented by H. S. Jones (Oxford: Clarendon Press, 1940; *Supplement*, 1968).

prototypes as and when they are necessary.[18] Although this point was not made explicit in *Structural Semantics* (indeed I could not honestly claim to have appreciated its significance), it is compatible with the way the results of the analysis were presented; and I shall take it for granted here. I will show how what appears to be the focal, or prototypical, meaning of certain Greek words was extended in a particular direction by Plato by the application of systematic and statable principles. In doing so, I will also suggest, though more tentatively and in this respect definitely going beyond, if not actually contradicting, what was said in *Structural Semantics*, that the three kinds of knowledge given lexical recognition in Greek correspond prototypically, though not in extension, to three different kinds of knowledge distinguished in modern philosopical discussion. The focal meaning of a word is revealed in, though not of course to be identified with, its most frequent or most characteristic collocations.[19] It is also the meaning that the native speaker would think of first and would find easiest to exemplify. I will not enter here into the methodological problems of applying these criteria in respect of the analysis of a closed corpus in a dead language. The question is, up to a point, dealt with in *Structural Semantics* and sufficient evidence is there presented (with references to the text) for those who know Greek to evaluate the analysis from a methodological point of view.

3. The field of knowledge and understanding in Platonic Greek

As there are three lexemes that cover the field of knowledge and understanding, according to Trier, in Middle High German, so there are three nouns that dominate what is identifiable intuitively as the same field in Platonic Greek: 'tekhne', 'episteme' and 'sophia'. They are conventionally translated into English by means of the words 'art', 'knowledge' (or 'science') and 'wisdom', respectively. But these translations, though

---

[18] Cf B. Berlin and P. Kay, *Basic Color Terms* (Berkeley & Los Angeles: Univ of Chicago Press, 1969); E. Rosch, 'Natural Categories', *Cognitive Psychology*, 4 (1973); H. Putnam, 'The Meaning of "Meaning"', in K. Gunderson (ed), *Language, Mind and Knowledge*, Minnesota Studies in the Philosophy of Science, 7, 1975 (reprinted in Putnam, *Mind, Language and Reality*, Cambridge: Cambridge UP); C. J. Fillmore, 'Topics in lexical semantics', in R. Cole (ed), *Current Issues in Linguistic Theory* (Bloomington, Ind: Indiana UP, 1977).

[19] Cf W. Haas, 'Semantic Value', *Proceedings of the Ninth International Congress of Linguistics* (Cambridge, Mass: Harvard UP, 1962).

satisfactory enough in certain contexts, are quite misleading in others. The opposition that holds in English between 'art' and 'science' did not hold between 'tekhne' and 'episteme' in Greek: on the contrary, there are many passages in Plato where 'tekhne' and 'episteme' are used interchangeably and with what appears to be the same meaning. (In making this statement, I tacitly accept that there is such a thing as context-dependent synonymy.) As far as 'sophia' is concerned, this denotes, not only wisdom, but also intelligence, cleverness, skill, etc; and there are passages where 'sophia' alternates with either 'episteme' or 'tekhne'. And yet 'tekhne', 'episteme' and 'sophia' are not synonymous in all contexts. What then is their meaning?

Let us start with 'tekhne'. This can be used, like the English word 'art' or 'science', but unlike 'knowledge', with either divided or undivided reference (ie as either a countable or an uncountable noun): one can be said to have tekhne or some particular tekhne; and, since 'tekhne' can be employed either collectively in the singular or distributively in the plural (again like 'art' or 'science'), particular tekhnes can be described either as parts of tekhne in general or alternatively as different kinds of tekhne. As different kinds, or parts, of science are institutionalized and given lexical recognition in the culture in which Modern English operates (physics, chemistry, biology, etc), so different kinds, or parts, of tekhne were institutionalized in fifth-century BC Athenian culture and given lexical recognition in Platonic Greek: pottery, medicine, farming, astronomy, gymnastics, weaving, etc. It will be obvious from these examples that tekhne, in so far as it relates to institutionalized occupations, includes much that we would distinguish in terms of 'art', 'science', 'craft', 'trade', etc. No such distinction is valid for Platonic Greek.

Correlated with the noun 'tekhne' (in the way that 'scientist' is correlated with 'science', or 'doctor' with 'medicine') is the morphologically unrelated 'demiourgos'. This is commonly glossed with 'craftsman'. Now, it is quite possible that the focal meaning of 'demiourgos' is narrower than that of 'tekhne', but anyone who plies or practises (epitedeuein), or simply has (ekhein), a particular tekhne is by virtue of that fact a demiourgos. And if he is good at this tekhne, he will be tekhnikos.

The adjective 'tekhnikos', which, when it is applied to a person, can be said to mean "having tekhne", is but one of more than four hundred semantically and, for the most part, morphologically related adjectives —let us call them T-adjectives — used by Plato. Some of these T-adjectives were, as far as we know, created by him to label a non-focal extension of 'tekhne' beyond its institutionalized prototypes. We shall look presently at the structural principles upon which these non-focal extensions are based. Here it may be observed that T-adjectives can be applied either to the person who has a particular tekhne or to the tekhne itself. It is as if we could apply the adjective 'agricultural' in English both to farmers and to farming. If 'agricultural' could be employed, in these circumstances, in the same way and with the same implications as one of the T-adjectives could be used in Greek, to say of someone that he was agricultural would be to imply that he was good at farming (good at his tekhne) and that he had (the) agricultural tekhne.

Enough has been said to show how 'tekhne' in its focal, or prototypical, meaning relates to Greek culture of the period and to a few of the other words in the field of knowledge and understanding. But how does 'tekhne' relate semantically to 'episteme' and 'sophia'? To answer this question we must now switch our attention to the verbs 'epistasthai', 'eidenai' and 'gignoskein', all of which are more or less satisfactorily translated by means of the single English verb 'know'.

Various kinds of knowledge have been recognized by modern epistemologists: notably, (1) knowledge-by-acquaintance; (2) knowledge-how-to (know-how); (3) propositional knowledge (knowing that something is or is not so). For reasons that I will not go into here, I will refer to these as knowledge$_1$, knowledge$_2$ and knowledge$_3$, respectively.[20] Knowledge$_1$ is manifest most characteristically in our ability to recognize and re-identify persons and things that we have previously encountered; knowledge$_2$, in our ability to perform certain acts or activities, such as throwing a pot or driving a car; and knowledge$_3$, in our ability to assert and vouch for propositions that we hold to be true.

Up to a point, the semantic difference between the Greek verbs 'gignoskein', 'epistasthai' and 'eidenai' can be explained in these terms. Their relative frequency of occurrence in collocation with particular classes of nominals in object position would support the view that 'gignoskein' means, prototypically or focally, "know$_1$", that 'epistasthai' means

[20] J. Lyons, 'Knowledge and Truth; a localistic approach', in D. J. Allerton, E. Carney and D. Holdcroft (eds), *Function and Context in Linguistic Analysis* (Cambridge: Cambridge UP, 1979).

"know$_2$" and that 'eidenai' means "know$_3$". 'Gignoskein' is the only one of the three verbs that is employed normally and frequently with a person-referring nominal as its direct object; 'epistasthai' is the only one that regularly takes an infinitive; and 'eidenai' occurs far more frequently with the equivalent of an English *that*-clause as its object than it does in any other construction.[21] In such contexts 'gignoskein' is satisfactorily translated by French 'connaître', German 'kennen', Polish 'znać', etc; 'epistasthai', by French 'savoir', German 'können', Polish 'umieć', etc; and 'eidenai', by French 'savoir', German 'wissen', Polish 'wiedzieć', etc. But there are two major qualifications that must be made to the statement that 'gignoskein', 'epistasthai' and 'eidenai' always mean, respectively, "know$_1$", "know$_2$" and "know$_3$".

First, 'epistasthai' is never used in respect of an unlearned ability. The systematic reflection of this is the relation of consequence that holds between the disjunction of 'manthanein' ("learn") and 'zetein' ("study", "enquire"), on the one hand, and 'epistasthai', on the other. This structural relation of sense can be represented formally in terms of a modified Carnapian meaning postulate (see point (v) of the previous section) which makes use of restricted variables and takes due account of the aspectual character of the verbs in question. To put it informally, and somewhat crudely, in our extended English metalanguage, if someone T-knows something (where the verb 'T-know' has the same meaning as the Greek 'epistasthai'), he must have acquired that knowledge by means of systematic study under a teacher or on his own. (It is interesting to note in this connection that knowledge of foreign languages falls within the scope of 'T-knowledge', but knowledge of one's native language, apparently, does not. One is tempted to say that this is because the ability to speak one's native language is seen as being natural, not learned. There is a certain amount of evidence to support this hypothesis and, as far as I am aware, nothing to disconfirm it.)

This feature of the meaning of 'epistasthai' holds in all contexts, not only in those in which it is used with an infinitival object. It is in this respect that 'epistasthai' differs semantically from both 'eidenai' and 'gignoskein', in contexts in which all three verbs are syntactically acceptable. For example, all three verbs might be applied in respect of one's knowledge of a poem or

[21] Cf Lyons, *Structural Semantics*, p 182.

a song. But if one used 'epistasthai', this would imply a deeper knowledge of the poem or the song than would the use of either 'gignoskein' or 'eidenai'; it would imply the ability to recite it, to explain its meaning, etc, and not merely the ability to recognize it. Although there is no reason to say that 'epistasthai' has two senses (that it sometimes means "know" and sometimes means "understand") it is often better translated into English with the verb 'understand' than it is by means of the verb 'know'. The second qualification that must be made to the statement that the three verbs mean severally "know$_1$", "know$_2$" and "know$_3$" is that, in contexts in which all three are syntactically acceptable, 'eidenai' (focally "know$_3$") is substitutable, *salva veritate*, for either 'epistasthai' (focally "know$_2$") or 'gignoskein' (focally "know$_1$"), whereas 'gignoskein' and 'epistasthai' are never intersubstitutable without change of meaning. As we have just seen, 'epistasthai' is used, in such contexts as elsewhere, to refer to knowledge (or understanding) that derives from systematic study: we have called this T-knowledge, because, as will be made clear presently, 'epistasthai' is relatable in a particular way to 'tekhne'. 'Gignoskein', on the other hand, denotes the kind of knowledge — let us call it, mnemonically, G-knowledge — that one either has naturally or acquires by way of a sudden insight or realization: indeed, in the aorist-perfective aspect (traditionally referred to as the aorist tense) it is often better translated by 'realize' or 'recognize' than it is by 'know' (cf the perfective of the Russian 'znatj'). 'Eidenai' — which refers, let us say, to E-knowledge — is more general than either 'epistasthai' or 'gignoskein' and can, for that reason, be used, in contextually appropriate circumstances, with the more specific implications of either. (As far as Plato's usage is concerned, there is no reason to say that 'gignoskein' is used for the kind of knowledge that comes from observation and 'eidenai' for knowledge resulting from reflection.[22] It is of course possible that for other authors or other periods a semantic distinction of this kind is justifiable.)

Let us now return to the nouns that are used to refer to knowledge and understanding. We will leave 'sophia' out of account for the moment: 'sophia', it will be recalled, is conventionally, and in certain contexts satisfactorily, translated with 'wisdom'. Now, it is readily demonstrated (though the standard dictionaries do not make this explicit) that, despite the

[22] Cf Liddell and Scott, *op cit*, p 350.

morphological relationship that holds between 'epistasthai' and 'episteme', the verb with which 'episteme' is most closely related semantically is 'eidenai' (to which we have tentatively assigned the focal, or prototypical, meaning "$know_3$"): it is 'tekhne' that goes with 'epistasthai' (tentatively "$know_2$"). In both cases, the semantic relation can be made explicit by means of a subjective or objective nominalization which holds constant the other lexical expressions.

To put it informally, if 'X epistasthai Y' is well formed, so too is both the subjective 'X's tekhne' and the objective 'Y's tekhne' (cf English 'John's knowledge' and 'the knowledge of geometry', respectively — but there is no equivalent in Greek of the English distinction between the inflectional and non-inflectional possessive). Similarly, if 'X eidenai Y' is well formed, so too is 'X's episteme' and 'Y's episteme'. Furthermore, for any well-formed 'X epistasthai Y', when Y is either an infinitive or one of a particular subset of non-personal nominals, there is a corresponding well-formed '(the) T-adjective tekhne', where a T-adjective is one of the morphologically productive adjectives referred to earlier, related to the headnoun of Y. It is as if — to take the same English example as before — from 'X T-knows agriculture/farming' one could derive '(the) agricultural tekhne' and, by a morphologically productive process, an indefinitely large number of nominals with the structure '(the) T-adjective tekhne'.

In all the resultant expressions, 'episteme' can be substituted for 'tekhne', preserving not only grammaticality, but also meaning, in contexts like 'X has (the) T-adjective tekhne/episteme'. Many of the T-adjectives are well established in the lexicon, and of frequent occurrence in Plato and other authors; very many others, however, are created by Plato by means of a productive adjectivalizing transformation in his discussion of the different kinds, or parts, of tekhne and episteme. The relation that holds between 'epistasthai' and 'tekhne' on the one hand, and the relation that holds between 'tekhne' and T-adjectives, on the other, supply Plato with the principle by virtue of which he is able to extend 'tekhne' beyond its institutionalized prototypes. It will now be clear why 'epistasthai' was said earlier to refer to T-knowledge (ie tekhne) and 'eidenai' to E-knowledge (ie episteme). On the assumption that 'eidenai', 'epistasthai' and 'gignoskein' have as their focal meanings, respectively, "$know_3$", "$know_2$" and "$know_1$", we must presently enquire how E-knowledge relates to $knowledge_3$, T-knowledge to $knowledge_2$ and G-knowledge to $knowledge_1$.

The intersubstitutability of 'episteme' and 'tekhne' is context-dependent; and this is consistent with the context-dependent intersubstitutability of the corresponding verbs. In short, 'episteme' and 'eidenai' are applied in respect of all kinds of knowledge, whereas 'tekhne' and 'epistasthai' are restricted to the kind of knowledge, skill or understanding (T-knowledge) that comes from systematic study and is manifest prototypically in the practice of institutionalized tekhnes; 'episteme' can be substituted, *salva veritate*, for 'tekhne' and (subject to certain syntactic constraints) 'eidenai' for 'epistasthai' in any context in which it is clear that the kind of knowledge that is relevant is tekhne.

There is no noun that stands in exactly the same relation to 'gignoskein' as 'episteme' and 'tekhne' do to 'eidenai' and 'epistasthai', respectively. The noun 'gnosis' is relatable syntactically and semantically to 'gignoskein'. But it differs in aspectual character from 'episteme' and 'tekhne': unlike them, it tends to be used to refer to an act (or event), rather than to a state. (This difference in aspectual character between 'gnosis' and 'episteme' or 'tekhne' is comparable with the difference between, let us say, 'realization', or 'recognition', and 'knowledge', in English: realization, like gnosis, happens or occurs, whereas knowledge, like tekhne or episteme, exists.) However, when due allowance is made for this difference in aspectual character, we can say that 'gnosis' is indeed the noun that goes with 'gignoskein': it is therefore appropriate to relate both 'gignoskein' and 'gnosis' to what we have been distinguishing as G-knowledge. (It may be added that the noun 'gnome', despite its morphological relationship with 'gignoskein', is synchronically closer in meaning to 'doxa' ("opinion", "belief") than it is to any word in the field of knowledge and understanding. It certainly does not denote G-knowledge.)

We come finally to 'sophia' and the corresponding adjective 'sophos'. It has already been mentioned that 'sophia' is frequently used in place of 'episteme' or 'tekhne'. How do we account for this fact? Briefly and informally: anyone who is particularly good at his tekhne or anyone who has any kind of knowledge or any kind of (what we would describe as) intellectual ability that would raise him above the average, will be, by that very token, sophos; and he will be more or less sophos to the degree that he is superior to the average person in respect of the knowledge, understanding or ability that he has.

There is also the further point to be made that 'sophos' and 'sophia' are closely related in Platonic usage to the more general words 'agathos' ("good") and 'arete' ("goodness", "virtue"). Sophia is a particular kind of goodness; it is, in fact, one of the four culturally recognized cardinal virtues, which are to some

G

degree inborn, but which can, and should, be cultivated by anyone striving for (what we would call) moral perfection. Classical scholars have long been aware of the difficulty, and at times the impossibility, of distinguishing between the moral and the intellectual (and the aesthetic) in the Greek scale of values. Porzig appears to have been right when he said: 'Man kann ganz allgemein sagen, dass die altgriechischen Ausdrücke für das, was nach unserer Aufgliederung Verstandesleistungen sind, stets auch einen Teil des sittlichen Bereichs umfassen, also eines Bereichs, den wir dem des Verstandes gern entgegenstellen. Das Verständnis der platonischen Philosophie hängt an der Erkenntnis dieser eigentümlichen Gliederung — es ist ein vergebliches Bemühn, hier auf dem Wege der Übersetzung eindringen zu wollen'.[23] However that may be, there can be no question but that the internal structure of the lexical field which contains 'episteme', 'tekhne', 'sophia' and related lexemes in Platonic Greek is different from the structure of the lexical field that contains 'Wissen', 'Verstand', 'Kenntnis', 'Weisheit', etc, in Modern German or 'knowledge', 'understanding' and 'wisdom' in English.

4. General conclusions

The results of the analysis reported in *Structural Semantics*, some of which have been presented very informally in the previous section, confirm, to my mind, the general validity of the point of view associated with the theory of semantic fields as this has been expounded, in several of his works, by the late Professor Ullmann. Indeed, there is a striking, if partial, similarity between Trier's representation of the field structured by 'wîsheit', 'kunst' and 'list' in Middle High German of about AD 1200 and my representation of the field structured by 'sophia', 'tekhne' and 'episteme'. As 'wîsheit' can be used in place of either 'kunst' or 'list', so 'sophia' can be employed instead of either 'tekhne' or 'episteme'; as 'wîsheit' refers to the kind of moral and intellectual perfection to which everyone, whatever his station in life, should aspire, so too does 'sophia' (due allowance being made for the cultural differences between fifth-century BC Greece and thirteenth-century AD Germany). So much for the similarities. The obvious difference is that, whereas 'kunst' and 'list' are in

---

[23] W. Porzig, *Das Wunder der Sprache* (Berne: Francke, 1950) pp 63–4.

contrast, 'tekhne' and 'episteme' are not; and the principal division in Platonic Greek, as we have seen, is not between two kinds of socially distinguishable knowledge or understanding, but between the knowledge (and understanding) that comes as a result of systematic study and the kind of knowledge that does not — between T-knowledge and G-knowledge, both of which are subsumed by the more inclusive E-knowledge.

It will be clear from what was said in the previous section, however, that the structure of the lexical field with which we have been concerned is not as sharply delineated as the brief and selective summary of the results that has just been given would suggest. Critics of the Trier-Weisgerber tradition of semantic analysis have frequently pointed out that the theory of semantic fields tends to exaggerate the orderliness and generality of the principles which determine the lexical structure of a language. On the basis of my own analysis of Platonic vocabulary in the field of knowledge and understanding, I would accept that this criticism is well founded. Nevertheless, subject to the qualifications that have been indicated in the previous section, generalizations of the kind that are made by scholars working in the Trier-Weisgerber tradition (or within the framework of some other version of post-Saussurean structural semantics) can be validly made and are, I submit, open to empirical confirmation or disconfirmation. Furthermore, they can be made in terms of meaning postulates established for particular languages, operating in their normal cultural setting, without the postulation of a metaphysically or psychologically prior conceptual content-substance and without the employment of a metalinguistic vocabulary of semantic components.

In this informal and very brief presentation of the results of the analysis reported in *Structural Semantics*, I have not been able to provide anything like a full statement of the syntagmatic relations that are important for the description of the field of 'tekhne', 'episteme' and 'sophia'. Enough information has been given, however, to make it clear that one cannot investigate the paradigmatic relations of sense without simultaneously taking into account the syntagmatic dimension. I must ask the reader to accept that a good deal more could have been said on this score.

In conclusion, I want to take up the question of the prototypical, or focal, meaning of the words in the field of knowledge and understanding with which we have been dealing (cf point (viii) of section 2). An appeal was made to the notion of focal meaning, in the previous section, in relation to institutionalized tekhnes, on the one hand, and to knowledge$_1$, knowledge$_2$ and knowledge$_3$, on the other. As far as these three kinds of knowledge are concerned, I have recently written about these elsewhere, without specific reference to Platonic Greek, but in a way which is consistent with, and in part derives from, the analysis summarized above.[24] For the present purpose, it will be sufficient to continue to identify knowledge$_1$ with knowledge-by-acquaintance, knowledge$_2$ with knowledge-how-to and knowledge$_3$ with propositional knowledge (knowledge-that). What I should like to suggest here is that, for a speaker of Attic Greek of Plato's time, there was implicit in his use of the relevant vocabulary items a distinction between G-knowledge and T-knowledge and that, whereas G-knowledge had knowledge-by-acquaintance (and recognition) as its single focal area (or prototype), T-knowledge had two intersecting focal areas, knowledge-how (the prototype for 'epistasthai') and institutionalized professional skill (the prototype for 'tekhne'). On the assumption that this was so, it is not difficult to see how the more general distinction that we have associated with the opposition between the two kinds of knowledge could have developed and been exploited by Plato. Admittedly, the trichotomy of knowledge-by-acquaintance, knowledge-how and knowledge-that, which I have tacitly taken to be universal, might well be attributed by a relativist to nothing more than the contingencies of the lexical and syntactic structures of particular languages. If this is in fact the case, it does not invalidate, as far as Platonic Greek is concerned, the suggestion that has just been made. However, present-day discussion of focal, or prototypical, meaning tends to be coupled with the assumption that it is universal (especially in respect of the denotation of natural kinds); and the very notion of the semantic prototype undoubtedly derives its attraction from the fact that it enables one to combine acceptance of a moderate version of universalism with a belief in the indeterminacy and ultimate untranslatability of lexical meaning.

[24] Cf Lyons, 'Knowledge and Truth', *op cit supra.*

Hypercharacterization of Pronominal Gender in Romance

YAKOV MALKIEL

Professor of Linguistics and Romance Philology, University of California, Berkeley

1. The Problem in Broad Outline

For those scholars (including the writer of these lines) who tend to assume that internal processes of language change, fundamentally, fall into three categories: increase of economy, sharpening of clarity, enhancement of expressivity, the basic problem in dealing with the hypercharacterization of morphological category (gender, case, or person, say) is to decide on the proper niche for it in that major edifice alluded to — unless it happens to straddle niches.

Hypercharacterization, at least in Indo-European, is rarely achieved through clipping, modern English being a notable exception from this pattern. Thus, economy hardly qualifies as a typical speech community's principal or exclusive goal in hypercharacterizing a given word or string of words. Clarity, conversely, may very well be at issue — as a matter of fact, on two levels: as regards either (a) the outer configuration of words (differentiation of forms) or (b) their referential or semantic load (heightened specification of meaning; in extreme cases, disambiguation). Expressivity, whether phonosymbolic or morphosymbolic,[1] clearly controls, and is in turn dependent on, hypercharacterization. To this extent, then, a collection of papers on semantics and style is one of the most appropriate contexts in which an advocate of analyses involving hypercharacterization may ask for a hearing.

There is no compelling reason for offering here any wealth of illustrations, for these can be easily culled from an earlier and far more circumstantial inquiry, entitled 'Diachronic Hypercharacterization in Romance'. Whatever

---

[1] On the possibility and wisdom of operating with a category of change worthy of this label see my own recent paper (1977: 511–29) and some reverberations in David Justice's forthcoming note.

the possible merits and certain shortcomings of that earlier piece, conceived
and written almost a quarter of a century ago, it seems to have sufficiently
aroused and satisfied the curiosity of my late colleague Stephen Ullmann for
him to have accepted it for publication, its length notwithstanding, in his
prestigious *Archivum Linguisticum*, where he spread it over two successive
fascicles.[2] The bipartition was justified for, after discussing the chosen
phenomenon in fairly general terms, I concentrated on the hypercharacterization of gender with special emphasis on the feminine (in nouns).
The other varieties of hypercharacterization remain, then, so many
adjoining fields left untilled; the one that clamours for immediate attention
continues the discussion of gender, chiefly however with a switch to the
masculine and the neuter (this time in pronouns and related categories, eg
the definite article). The residual survival of the neuter in the ranks of
Romance pronouns is a well-established fact, familiar to every tyro of
language-learning, to say nothing of historical linguistics; but the specifics
of various speech communities' sporadic attempts to draw a line, or even
drive a wedge, between masculine and neuter have not yet, I suspect, been
effectively examined in this particular perspective.[3] The feminine will
occasionally come up for mention, without monopolizing our curiosity any
longer.

2.   From OPtg. *esto, esso, . . . todo* to Mod. *isto, isso, . . . tudo*

Even superficial familiarity with contemporary Spanish and Portuguese
suffices to recognize a cleavage between these two languages as regards
certain pronouns which perform adjectival services as well. The Spanish
demonstrative series (m.) *este,* (f.) *esta,* (n.) *esto* corresponds to Ptg. *êste,
esta, isto,* and in the plural (m.) *estos,* (f.) *estas* clash with *êstes, estas.* Exactly
the same contrasts prevail in the two parallel series, endowed with different

---

[2] This article of mine, published over twenty years ago (1957: 79–113, 1958: 1–36), is now best
consulted in the translation into Italian we owe to Olga Devoto and Ruggero Stefanini, with
some additional illustrations thrown in for good measure (1970: 170–239). I am unaware of
any major critical reactions, but have myself used this approach on several subsequent
occasions.
[3] A short piece of my own, 'Deux frontières entre la phonologie et la morphologie en
diachronie' (1973: 79–87), can hardly be cited as an exception. Though I submitted this
invitational note in an impeccably neat typescript, it appeared with numerous misprints,
chiefly because I was denied the privilege of proofreading.

semantic overtones: (a) *ese, esa, eso, esos, esas* over against *êsse, essa, isso, êsses, essas* and (b) *aquel, aquella, aquello, aquellos, aquellas* in contradistinction to *aquêle, aquela, aquilo, aquêles, aquelas*. If one includes the classical literatures of these two cultures in one's purview, one can expand this corpus by culling from the texts two more such series: (c) *aqueste, aquesta, aquesto,* etc vs. *aquêste, aquesta, aquisto* etc; and (d) *aques(s)e, aques(s)a, aques(s)o,* etc vs. *aquêsse, aquessa,* and perhaps *aquisso,* etc.[4] Furthermore, it is common knowledge, and was explicitly stated by J. Cornu as early as 1888, that the Ptg. set *todo, toda, tudo* exhibited a certain resemblance to the demonstratives in its opposition to Sp. (m. and n.) *todo* alongside (f.) *toda;* no comparably sharp contrast could be detected in the respective plurals.

In turning to the historical analysis of these, all told, six series, one observes at once that Sp. *estos, esos* reflect the last syllable of their etymon Lat. *istōs, ipsōs* far better than do Ptg. *êstes, êsses*. In the array of 3rd sg. and pl. personal pronouns, the discrepancy repeats itself: Sp. *ellos* echoes Lat. *illōs* more faithfully than does Ptg. *êles*, a fact relevant in this context on account of the similarly erratic distribution of Sp. *aquellos* and Ptg. *aquêles*. The fact that Spanish has been satisfied with persevering where Portuguese has aimed at innovating is extraordinarily interesting and leads us to wonder in what direction the Portuguese speech community was striking out.

Historical grammar, in this connection, has served as a real eye-opener. Even the pioneering treatises by K. von Reinhardstoettner and J. Cornu (ordinarily less than satisfactory on account of the inadequate sources tapped) established the crucial fact that medieval texts from Portugal, in the singular, favoured the series *este, esta, esto; esse, essa, esso; todo, toda,* etc.[5] To this day scholars entertain doubts as to whether the stressed vowels of, say, *este, esta, esto,* traceable to the same Latin source *(ĭ),* were differentiated

[4] For a scrupulously documented Spanish collection of data one turns best to the torso of Keniston's magnum opus (1937; see the Index [713b] for further guidance to the relevant paragraphs). *Aques(t)e,* etc display an unmistakable side-connection to certain adverbs and prepositions, such as *aquí, acá* (also spelled *aquá*), *aquende,* while *aquel* has a parallel link to *allí, allende.*

[5] See K. von Reinhardstoettner (1878: §§120, 145), who fell back on such data as he could carve from Frei Joaquim de Santa Rosa de Viterbo's *Elucidário . . .,* F. A. von Varnhagen's *Trovas e cantares . . .* (1849), and T. Braga's *Antologia portuguesa* (1876). J. Cornu, *Die portugiesische Sprache* (1888, 1904–06: §314) identified neither his primary nor his secondary sources.

throughout the Middle Ages. But even without such differentiation the endings fully sufficed to keep apart the masculines (*este, esse, -ele*) from the neuters (*esto, esso, -elo*). This weak differentiation Old Portuguese shared with Old Castilian and other medieval Peninsular dialects.

Toward the end of the Middle Ages Portuguese began to move in a direction which was to separate it sharply from Spanish. For the neuters, the unequivocal spellings *isto, isso, -ilo* began to make their appearance, competing for a while with *esto*, etc. In the ranks of the feminines, one infers on circumstantial evidence, the tendency to substitute /ɛ/ for inherited /e/ began to assert itself, so that *esta, essa* ceased to be pronounced, as they initially doubtless had been, [estɐ], [esɐ] and became instead [ɛstɐ], [ɛsɐ] and, eventually, [ɛʃtɐ], [ɛsɐ] — which is today's Lisbonese and Carioca pronunciation. Through a sort of symmetric, or sympathetic, gambit, *o* was raised to *u* in the neuter of *todo*, which was thus transmuted into *tudo*. Nevertheless, the present-day series *todo, toda, tudo* resembles only in part *êste, esta, isto*, inasmuch as the stem-syllable *o*'s of *todo* and *toda* have remained undifferentiated (in dramatic contrast to those of the numerous adjectives in *-oso* /ozu/, *-osa* /ɔzɐ/, such as *formoso, -osa* 'shapely, beautiful') and, furthermore, inasmuch as the masculines and the neuters, for once, show not a trace of the characteristic alternation *-e* : *-o*.

To put it differently: The three genders inherited from the Latin pronouns *(iste, ista, istud)* were, from the start, nicely distinguished in Luso- and Hispano-Romance; but speakers of Portuguese, in the last seven centuries or so, have gone overboard to exaggerate this distinction, ending up with a unique three-way pattern: /ɛ/, /e/, /i/, a truly perfect example of hypercharacterization of gender. The development of *todo* has been far less radical than that of the demonstratives.

Such is the main thrust of the evolution. There have occurred all sorts of delays and accelerations on the dialect level, as when OPtg. (n.) *todo* has lingered on in certain varieties of Galician or as when several Galician dialects, in the end, have allowed the innovative stressed *i* to spread to the ranks of masculines and feminines.[6] These ramifications, for all their

---

[6] Judging from Crespo Pozo's succinct indications, at present *aquel, aquella, aquello* prevail in the provinces of Pontevedra and La Coruña, whereas *aquil*, etc predominate in Orense and Lugo (1963: 79). The author lists only *todo*, to the exclusion of any *-u-* variant (621).

pertinence, cannot long hold our attention here; neither can we indulge any leisurely inventorying of scattered traces of *aqueste, aquesse,* and related forms jettisoned by the literary language.[7] Finally, any discussion of the possible relation between syntactic devices (eg *lo sé todo* 'I know everything') in Spanish as near-equivalents of Portuguese morphological innovations *(todo > tudo)* must be postponed.

The mosaic of survivals, shifts, and adjustments to new conditions which has here been pieced together gives the impression of a cogent enough reconstruction, and the basic facts have indeed, one hopes, been irreversibly established. But as one's attention turns to the elucidation of forces that must have been at work to produce so many and such diversified changes, one discovers before long rather embarrassing disagreements among experts, to the extent that they have at all been willing to commit themselves to some specific explanation, rather than invoking unknown or obscure forces, in a fit of agnosticism.[8] A few examples must suffice. K. von Reinhardstoettner (1878: §120), for instance, knew a good deal about *esto, esso, todo,* etc, as forerunners and, in the end, rivals of mod. *isto, isso, tudo,* but drew very infelicitous conclusions from his observations of details, as when he argued that the older language displayed a particular tendency toward explicitly neuter forms ('die ältere Sprache zeigte . . . bisweilen das Streben nach einer neutralen Form') when, in reality, it was the more modern stage that excelled in the marking of the neuter gender. Equally baffling is that pioneer's confusion of (a) petrifacts of Latin neuter pronouns in Portuguese, such as *al* 'something else' and *algo* 'something' (from *alid* and *ali-quid* or *-quod,* respectively) and the development of the

---

[7] Another side-issue that cannot be gone into here is the sporadic aphaeresis of the opening vowel; Reinhardstoettner pointed out scattered traces of *sto, questo* in Old Portuguese. If Bernardim Ribeiro, at the threshold of Renaissance literature, still wrote: *aqueste meu mal contar; quando lhe eu aquisto ouvi,* there are no longer any vestiges of this set of demonstratives left in Galician, judging from the silence of L. Carré Alvarellos. Interestingly, Judaeo-Spanish, as recorded before World War II in Bucharest and Skoplje, tended, in Italian fashion, to use not only the same stem vowel, but also the same ending for masculine and neuter, allowing *esto* here and there to correspond to both Stand. Sp. *este* and *esto*; cf Crews (1935: §§41, 1184).

[8] One of the worst offenders, in this respect, was J. J. Nunes, who bluntly declared: '. . . a passagem que ainda não foi satisfactòriamente explicada do *e* tónico para *i*' (1919: 248). Seventeen years later, M. Rodrigues Lapa, in concluding his lengthy review of *Altportugiesisches Elementarbuch* (see below), castigated J. Huber for the latter's restraint from explicative commitments.

neuter as a live force.[9] J. Cornu (1888, 1904–06: §§314, 318) dropped no explicative remarks, but observed that, as late as the 15th century, *esto*, etc, surpassed *isto*, etc, in sheer frequency of incidence; also, that *isto* and *isso* paved the way for *aquil(l)o* and the rest. Cornu further included in his purview OPtg. *peroo* = *peró* 'but', on account of its background *(per hoc)*. García de Diego, as an explorer of Galician (c1908: 60), was aware of the vital importance of the shift *e* > *i*, but drew a completely distorted picture of the sequence of events, contending that the metaphonically raised vowel came into existence in the masculine, then spread to the other genders, and ultimately remained only in the ranks of the neuter. Dunn (1928: §§300–302) gave an excellent phraseological account of *isto é* 'that is to say', *nisto* 'meanwhile', 'then, at such a moment, thereupon', *por isto* (= *por isso*) 'therefore', *não* (or *nem*) *por isso* 'in spite of that', 'not so much', 'please' — but curbed the temptation of offering genetic explanations. Huber, in the wake of Carolina Michaëlis, assiduously studied Old Portuguese rhymes, documenting, eg, *tudo : perdudo* and *tudo : conhoçudo* as well as *isto : Antecristo*; then, too, he cited dated charters, pushing back the rise of certain metaphonized pronouns to the 13th century (*isto*: AD 1270, 1276; *aquilo*: AD 1214). But side by side with such useful shreds of information (1933: §§87, 349) Huber indulged the luxury of inexcusably reckless conjectures, as when he mused that the high vowels of OPtg. *usso* alongside *osso* 'bear' < *ŭrsu*, *tudo* (AD 1262) alongside *todo* 'everything' < *tōtu*, and *migo* 'with me', *nusco* 'with us', etc, as so many echoes of *mēcum*, *nō(bi)scum*, etc, might conceivably have been generated by word-final -*o* < Lat. -*u* (§97:2). It goes without saying that *usso* was a compromise between learnèd *urso* and vernacular *osso* (the leaning toward a Latinism having been provoked by taboo, cf It. *lupo* 'wolf'); that OPtg. *mego* 'with me' < *mēcum* was flanked by *migo*, which simply reflected the substitution of *mí* < *mihī* for the descendant of *mē* which prevailed elsewhere (Fr. *moi*, etc); and that the rivalry of *nosco* and *nusco* echoed, through symmetrical development, the competition between *mego* and *migo*, all of which knocks any foundation from under the interpretation of *tudo* (AD 1202) from *todo* < *tōtu* as metaphonic, hence essentially phonetic. I do not know whether Leite de

---

[9] The author's worst blunder, on balance, was his remark: 'Der neutrale Begriff wird durch die maskuline Form dargestellt, z.B. *o formoso* "das Schöne" . . . wo die spanische Sprache noch den Artikel *lo* hat.' As I shall attempt to show farther down, Sp. *lo hermoso*, far from representing a relic, constitutes a bold innovation.

Vasconcelos' enormous, far-flung *œuvre* contains any synthesis of the many excellent observations scattered over his writings with respect to the problem under scrutiny; among other points that he made, in part on the basis of his own field-work, let me mention his discovery of Trasm. (Moncorvo) *(a)quisso* and of *d'aquisso, por quisso* 'd'aquilo, disso, por isso' as well as of (f.) *aquessa* in the Concelho de Castel Branco and in the Alto Alentejo.[10] Though perfectly aware of the spread of the radical *i* to other genders in modern Galician *(iste, ise, il),*[11] Leite was cautious enough to interpret *aquiles, istes* in a Portuguese charter of the year 1262 as due to deliberate Latinization on the part of the scribe, because he had detected, in the group of texts at issue, other vestiges of the same tendency.[12] Beyond correctly etymologizing OPtg. *peró* 'por isso, contudo', he unwittingly helped us, through his gloss, to understand why *tudo* joined the demonstratives in acquiring a hypercharacterized neuter: Common phrases, such as *por isso* and *contudo*, happened to be practically interchangeable. Finally, he provided for *aquest-e, -o* welcome documentation from the *Cancioneiro da Vaticana* and from the *Cancioneiro d'el-Rei Denis*, as reconstructed by Henry R. Lang.[13]

In her Glossary to the *Cancioneiro da Ajuda*, published in 1920 but compiled at the peak of her career (*c*1906), Carolina Michaëlis de Vasconcelos, under several important entries (*aquelo, aquesto, aquisto, esso, esto, isto*, etc), made statements which in the aggregate constitute a synopsis of the history of demonstratives. She documented, conceivably for the first

---

[10] One finds shreds of this information in several of the author's writings, including the précis of his lecture courses (1911: 57, 1926: 55–7, 1959: 52–5) and his anthology of archaic texts (1907: 125).

[11] See (1907: 125b, 132b; 1926: 57). Like Carolina Michaëlis at approximately the same time, Leite here believed in the agency of metaphony, stating with even superior explicitness: 'Isto é , por *illi* (com Umlaut) por influência de *qui*'.

[12] (1907: 125b). This is, clearly, not the same thing as charging the general change *e* > *i* in certain demonstratives to learned pressure, as was done (E. B. Williams reports) by Cavacas (1920: 139) and tentatively even by an expert of the stature of M. Rodrigues Lapa.

[13] It may some day be rewarding, in the light of our remarks on *tudo*, to explore whether the conspicuous m. pl. subj. *tuit* 'all' in Old French would not be best explained as an attempt, by speakers, to arrive at a distinctive subject-case form that represents a suitable counterpart to obj. *toz* < *tōt(t)ōs*, on the model of *cil* : *ceus* and *cist* : *cez*. Meyer-Lübke was quick to realize that such OFr. indefinites as *autrui* and *nului*, later *nelui*, echoed certain demonstratives, but he left *tuit*, an isolate, unexplained (1913: §276). If my surmise is correct, the sole difference between the two processes would consist in this: Although the pressure, in both languages, went in the same direction, it affected the singular in Portuguese and the plural in Old French.

time, (f.) *aquelha*, unmasking it as a camouflaged Hispanism; traced *isto* and *aquisto* to the chosen text, and *aquilo* to three passages of the *Grail* romance. Unfortunately, she invoked at least three times metaphony as the force behind such changes as *aquesto* > *aquisto, aquelo* > *aquilo,* and *esto* > *isto.* Worse, from the fact that some present-day Galician dialects exhibit the var. *tuido*, which doubtless arose under pressure from *muito* 'much', she drew the indefensible conclusion that the incomparably older shift *todo* > *tudo* must be similarly interpreted (1920: 89*a*).

On this side of the Atlantic, Edwin B. Williams cited a few by-forms overlooked or side-tracked in earlier discussions eg 'old and popular' *aquel* beside *aquele,* pl. *aqueis* alongside *aqueles* (1938, 1962–68: §145) and offered an excellent, if incomplete, synopsis of earlier analyses, ranging from a fledgeling Meyer-Lübke's far-fetched hypothesis of metaphony through /w/, as in *istu̦ es vero* (1890: §82) to a still young and inexperienced M. Rodrigues Lapa's conjecture of the impact of *aqui* on *aquesto,* which, after producing *aquisto,* allegedly led to *isto, isso,* and *aquilo* (1936: 304); philological evidence points to spread in the opposite direction. Unfortunately, the splendidly-informed Philadelphia scholar preferred to refrain from any commitment, as if to signal the message that he was unconvinced. In *tudo,* much worse, he recognized a regular sound development.

All difficulties are removed at one blow once we make a single assumption, namely that the Portuguese speech community, starting with the 12th or 13th century, began to hypercharacterize the three genders of certain pronouns, adding a novel pattern of differentiation of stem vowels to the preëxistent diversity of endings, which Old Portuguese from the start shared with Old Spanish. Had there been in existence a Western counterpart of Sp. *ello,*[14] namely **elo,* it would undoubtedly have undergone the change to **ilo.*

[14] On the finer points of the use and development of *ello* there are available to us the two studies by P. Henríquez Ureña (1939: 209–29; 1940: 226–30). By way of elaboration on them, in terms of contrastive rather than comparative analysis, one may ask oneself what, say, the Portuguese, the French, and the Italian translations of the illustrative sentences adduced by the author would sound like. Only very distantly related to the knotty problems here discussed is the protracted coexistence, in medieval and Golden Age Spanish, of *mesmo* and *mismo* 'self, same', inasmuch as these two variants both represented borrowings from Old French, where *mëesme* and *mëisme* corresponded, at the outset, to different declensional cases. It is not impossible that the eventual dislodgement of *mesmo* by *mismo* in post-Cervantian Spanish was conditioned by the *i*'s closer affinity with the following *-sm-* cluster. In Portuguese *mesmo* (orig. *meesmo*) won out, after ousting an autochthonous form, *medês* < *met ipse* (or *ipsu*), whose *-ês* component neatly matches the *-es-* ingredient of OFr. *mëesme.*

3. The Third-Person Personal Pronouns

Whereas the descendants of *iste* and *ipse* (plus those of *ille* if preceded by the deictic particle *ak-*) developed into two parallel series of demonstrative pronouns and adjectives, *ille* used in isolation, unheralded by such a particle, yielded entirely different products on Luso-Hispanic soil.[15] As heavily stressed words, *ille, illa, illu(d)* asserted themselves qua 3rd-ps. personal pronouns, 'he', 'she', and 'it', whereas as lightly stressed words, they gave rise to the definite articles, which thus turn out to have the flavour of extra-pale relational adjectives in Peninsular dialects. We shall first consider the services they have lent as personal pronouns, through suppletive interplay with the reflexes of *egō* 'I' and *tū* 'thou' beside *nōs* 'we' and *vōs* 'ye'.

Significantly, in the singular, judging from the masculine, the nominative case was adopted, witness Sp. *él, ella, ello* (Ptg. only *êle* and *ela*), while in the plural the oblique case, coinciding there historically with the accusative, prevailed (Sp. *ellos* < *illōs, ellas* < *illās*), except that Portuguese, as with *êste* and *êsse*, innovated by extending *-e,* in lieu of *-o,* to the plural. In archaic Spanish texts the forms (m. sg.) *elli, elle* dominated — a point scrutinized by Menéndez Pidal (1941: §93) and a few other workers of his generation. The distribution *elle : elli* was undoubtedly dialectal,[16] closely matching those of *este : esti, esse : essi,* and, in the ranks of 'strong' preterites (1st sg.), those of *fize : fizi* 'I did, made' *(<fēcī), vine :* *vini* 'I came' *(<vēnī),* and the like. On the strength of the latter parallel, there is little if any doubt that the actual starting points, in provincial Latin, were (m. sg.) **illī, *ipsī, *istī.* It is further clear that *elle/elli* became *él* via *ell* (cf OProv. *elh*), through apocope (as with *est*) and subsequent depalatalization of the lateral, as in *mílle* 'a thousand' > OSp. *mill* > mod.

---

[15] I incline to give a low assessment to the number of traces *ipse* has left in the Peninsula as the root of the definite article, except for the Balearic Zone. Elsewhere (1979: 1–36) I have substantiated my scepticism in regard to D. Alonso's interpretation (1943: 30–47) of dialectal *hasta sa(g)ora.*

[16] See the mutually complementary studies by G. Tilander (1937) and, on a higher level of sophistication, J. Gulsoy (1969), who is explicit, not to say emphatic, about the organic transmission of *ī*: '. . . the view which traces [-*i*] to *ī* in an unbroken line is incontrovertible' (183); 'B[erceo]'s *-i* < *-ī* involved an unbroken persistence of the Latin vowel' (187). Gulsoy adds to his arsenal of proofs the cases of sg. impt. *vivi* < *vīvī* and the conjunct pronouns *li(s)* < *illi(s).* As for *embaldi* 'in vain', *tardi* 'late', etc, where the models lacked *-ī,* it seems simplest to argue that each medieval dialect tended to generalize a single unstressed final front vowel: Castile opted for *-e,* while Alta Rioja banked on *-i.*

mil. But while all these details are either known or readily understandable within the frame of existing knowledge, the 'master-plan' behind all these individual gambits — choice of the nominative in preference to the accusative, preservation of the neuter in the singular, apocope, interplay between two classes of lateral consonants — remains hidden unless one assumes that a powerful trend toward hypercharacterization of pronominal gender was all the while at work. This tendency it was that must have prompted speakers to adopt **illī*, **istī*, **ipsī*, with a 'supernominative' ending for the masculine echoing, systemically, the final vowel of *quī* 'which'. The widespread explanation[17] to the effect that, say, *ille quī, iste quī*, etc, led to **illī quī*, **istī quī* through an essentially phonetic process of anticipatory vowel assimilation, in my estimate, makes very little sense, first because the sequences credited with having triggered the development were not particularly common or otherwise conspicuous in folk speech (or in other registers), and second because this kind of metaphony, across word borders, was thoroughly alien to most varieties of colloquial Latin. We are faced with an eloquent instance of paradigmatic, by no means with one of syntagmatic, adjustment.

The testimony of other Romance languages confirms this suspicion. Though Portuguese lacks a neuter comparable to Sp. *ello* (or to its own series *isto, isso, aquilo, tudo*), its speakers have overridden normal sound change and seen to it that the stem vowels of *êle* /e/ and *ela* /ɛ/ were effectively polarized; the opening of the stressed vowel in *ela* was clearly secondary. In Gallo-Romance, (m. sg.) **illī* cast off *il*,[18] which in modern

---

[17] I distinctly remember my first exposure to this doctrine in 1933, through lecture courses and proseminars; this experience, from the start, left me unconvinced. Discernibly more incisive was A. Darmesteter's and, independently, E. Herzog's conjecture, later endorsed by Meyer-Lübke (1913: §265), to the effect that the co-existence in spoken Latin of *quī, cūius, cuī* and *ille, illuius, illui* (in lieu of Classical gen. *illīus*, dat. *illī*) gave rise to sg. nom, *illī*. Meyer-Lübke thus espoused the paradigmatic thesis, without bothering to have recourse to that term or to toy with hypercharacterization; while giving credit to G. Rydberg for documenting *illī* in 6th-century Latin, he dissociated himself (loc. cit.) from the Swedish scholar's syntagmatic hypothesis, rejecting in the process also H. Schuchardt's alternative lexical solutions (*ille* × *hīc*, or *illīc* 'there' favoured as a substitute for *ille*).

[18] The hypercharacterization of pronominal gender was least strongly developed in Old Provençal which, puzzlingly enough, allowed the form *ilh* to occupy two slots: It functioned as the stressed m. pl. pronoun and as the f. sg. pronoun (both in the subject case); see Schultz-Gora (1911: §§114f) and Appel (1915: 364*b*, s.v. *el*). The former Provençalist offered a tentative explanation (the eviction of the rel. pron. *quae* by ambigeneric *quī* may have set in motion reverberations in the ranks of demonstratives). But since the finest troubadour poetry tolerated this bizarre ambiguity, the enthronement of the adored lady as the poet's feudal overlord may have had its share in this baffling development.

French contrasts elegantly with *elle*, on the level of polished speech: /il/ : /ɛl/ and, even more dramatically, on the plateau of folk-speech: /i/ : /ɛl/. In Old Tuscan, the opposition through contrastable endings: *ello* : *ella* or *elli* : *ella*, might have sufficed; however, the clash has been reinforced through adoption of *egli* with /ʎ/, under whichever circumstances, in lieu of expected *elli*;[19] thus the clash of the consonant pillars enhanced the opposition.

4. The Definite Article in Old Spanish

The use of the definite article in contemporary Spanish is easily capsulized into this set of examples: m. sg. *el* (*hermano* 'brother'), f. sg. *la* (*hermana* 'sister') beside f. *el* (*alma* 'soul') and n. *lo* (*bueno* 'good'); m. pl. *los* (*hermanos*), f. pl. *las* (*hermanas*). A certain symmetry prevails, strictly speaking, only between *la hermana* and *las hermanas*, with a neat marking of gender and number. *El* is extraordinarily ambiguous, prefixed as it is (a) to normally structured masculines, such as *hermano*; (b) to masculines displaying an ordinarily feminine ending, such as *el* (*día* 'day'), pl. *los* (*días*); and (c) to feminine nouns beginning with stressed *a*, such as *el* (*alma* 'soul'), pl. *las* (*almas*), to the exclusion of adjectives: *la* (*alta torre* 'high tower'). The so-called neuter *lo* heralds an adjective (*mío, bueno*), but not an ordinary noun, and admits of no plural, two restrictions which set apart Sp. *lo* from, say, G. *das*, or from the neuter endings *-um* and *-u* of Latin.

The farther back we go along the axis of time, the clearer the picture is apt to become. In Golden Age texts sequences like *el alta torre* were

---

[19] G. Rohlfs has assembled many interesting facts on the state of affairs in Old and Modern Italian (1949–54: §436), unfortunately without quite having managed to knit them together. Properly interpreted, these stray data bear out the assumption of progressive hyper-characterization of gender. *Ello* or *esso* 'he' vs *ella* or *essa* 'she' displayed only the normal degree of gender-distinction. OIt. *elli*, echoing *chi* < *quī*, beside *ella* exhibited a more dramatic contrast, and after the former had yielded to *egli* the additional clash of /ʎ/ and /l/ advantageously widened the gap. The tendential substitution of *lui* for *egli* and of *lei* for *ella* in the subject case worked in the same direction of steady polarization, even though other forces may also have been at work.

Rohlfs's argument in accounting for the shift *elli* > *egli* is typical of his (syntagmatic) modus operandi. The change, traceable to older literature, started, we learn, in prevocalic position (*elli amava*), where it was 'normal'. There follows a leap in Rohlfs's further chronicle of events: 'So wurde *egli* in moderner Zeit die herrschende Form des Schrifttums'. But this is a non sequitur, unless one hastens to add that a mere possibility was exploited to the hilt — in response to the craving for hypercharacterization.

tolerated; in the late Middle Ages *el* was found before any feminine noun beginning with a stressed vowel, not just before *á*: *el* (*ossa* 'female bear'), and in a still earlier period of time the qualification 'stressed' was not enforced: *el* (*amada* 'paramour'). Finally, we hit a stratum where prevocalic *el* appears under its pristine form *ell*: *ell alma, ell ermana*; simultaneously, the corresponding masculine definite article before vowel comes into view, also *ell*, thus: *ell* (*omne* 'man'), *ell ermano*. At that archaic stage, then, the forms of the definite article were: m. sg. *el, ell*; f. sg. *la, ell*; n. *lo*; m. pl. *los*; f. pl. *las*, and the connection with the demonstrative series *él, ella, ello, ellos, ellas* was distinctly more visible. From the syntagm *ell árvol* 'the tree' it was impossible to determine the gender of the noun, and the evidence of Ptg. *a árvore*, plus the gender of *arbor* in Classical Latin alert us to the possibility that *ell árvol*, for a while, was indeed feminine for many, if not most, speakers of Old Spanish.[20]

Within this motley picture we clearly recognize a small subset of forms beginning with *e-*, which reflects the *ĭ* of *ĭlle*, etc: *el, ell*; and a larger subset of forms marked by *l-*: *lo, la, los, las*. This diversity of shapes is usually explained by the various surgeries to which weakly stressed *ille* was subjected, according to syntactic and rhythmic conditions: *ĭl(le), ĭll(e); (ĭl)lu(d), (ĭl)lōs, (ĭl)lās*. The one feature that remains unexplained in this scheme is the polarization of *ĭl(le)* and *(ĭl)lu(d)*. Portuguese, eg, makes do with *o meu* = 'el mío' and 'lo mío', and the same holds for Fr. *le mien*, etc. There must have been a special force at work that, through use of different patterns of carving, produced the separate cuts *el* and *lo* in Old Spanish, with the added complication that pl. *los* matches sg. *el* rather than *lo*, an obvious liability of the system. The only force that could have rammed through this erratic sort of polarization was the tendency toward

---

[20] There have become available, by now, many shreds of carefully sifted information on the definite article in Luso- and Hispano-Romance, and a new synthesizing discussion of early phases is overdue, to replace E. Gamillscheg's Berlin Academy memoir (1936), which must be written off as a failure. One of the best treatments, prepared in the wake of R. Menéndez Pidal's and E. Staaff's pioneering efforts, we owe to R. Lapesa (1948: §25), who documented OAst. *ela, elos, elas* and disclosed the long coexistence of *el* and *lo* as articles, with slight contextual differentiation. In resuming their attack on this problem, scholars will do well to take into account certain conjunct forms of the personal pronouns, which in part outwardly coincide with those of the definite articles (Ptg. *o, a*, etc), in part, as clitics, preserve an archaic configuration (Ptg. *fazê-lo, dizemo-la*, etc), or else are innovative (Ptg. *trazem-nos* 'they carry them').

hypercharacterization of all three genders in Old Spanish pronouns, the drift toward a triadic arrangement.[21]

In the past, as a result of their cultural background, grammarians and 'philosophers of language' have, as a rule, focused attention on such uses of *lo* as *lo hermoso* 'the [essentially] beautiful', 'das Schöne [an sich]', in vivid recollection of Platonic ideas allegedly thus conveyed. In sober fact, modern Spanish resorts to *lo* on a far more generous scale in all sorts of adverbial phrases: (coll.) *a lo mejor* 'like as not', *a lo vivo* 'effectively', *dar (herir) en lo vivo* 'to touch (cut, hurt) to the quick', *a lo largo* 'lengthwise', where it competes, to some extent, with the *-as* forms: *a buenas* 'willingly', *de buenas a primeras* 'suddenly', *a malas* 'on bad terms', *(estar) de malas* 'out of luck'. Equally characteristic of the modern language is the exclamatory sequence *lo* + adv. or variable adj.: *¡lo bien que lo sabe!; ¡lo hermosa que está!* (in lieu of older *cuan*). All these century-old extensions are, to be sure, noteworthy, but must not blind one to the fact that, historically, the kernel of such uses, as observable in medieval texts, was the subset *lo mió* (later *mío*), *lo to* (later *túo* and, under the influence of *cuyo* 'whose', eventually *tuyo*), etc, over against which *lo ál* and *lo ageno* 'that which is not my (thy, etc) property' were minted as the semantic opposites. This state of affairs takes us back, not unexpectedly, to the confinement of the Romance neuter to pronouns. The genuine substantivated adjective in Spanish was either masculine or feminine, exactly as in the cognate languages, and was correspondingly ushered in, where any need for the definite article arose, by either *el* or *la*: *el largo* 'length', *la larga* 'long billiard cue'.

5. Animate vs Inanimate Indefinite Pronouns

From the lexical and grammatical resources bequeathed by late Antiquity the medieval Romance languages developed a mechanism for distinguishing, within the territory of certain indefinite pronouns, the animate from the inanimate subset (eg 'someone else' from 'something else'). Even

[21] The situation is discernibly simpler in Standard Catalan, where the forms for the masculine are (sg.) *el* and (pl.) *els*, and those for the feminine are (sg.) *la* and (pl.) *les*, the only deviation from this pattern being the elision of both *el* and *la* to *l'* before vowel — similarly to the French rule. Since 'the best thing' and 'the best (man)' are both, indistinguishably, *el millor* (= Sp. *lo mejor* and *el mejor*), one is left wondering why an aficionado grammarian, such as Joan Gili (1967: 25), should at all be operating with a 'neuter article . . . only used with adjectives, participles, etc'. *Lo, la,* etc are confined to the dialect level, quite apart from the survival of *su* and *sa,* from *ipsu, ipsa,* in the Balearic branch.

H

though gender is far from acting as the straight linguistic representation of sex, or so much as its oblique implication, it nevertheless is true that their domains overlap; and since sex has a bearing on the dichotomy animate vs inanimate, the remaining category of opposition, which lumps together masculine and feminine and pits them jointly against neuter, marginally lends itself to analysis within the frame of this paper.

Initially, the endings -*ī* (echoing *quī* 'who') and -*em* (extracted from *quem* 'whom') beside -*uī* (used in response to *cuī* 'to whom') were individuated as markers of case and served to buttress the collapsing or, at least, endangered positions of subject case and object (oblique) case. Thus, *alter* 'the other' (and, in provincial Vulgar Latin, also 'another') was sharpened, in its syntactic role of subject, through the use of **ált(e)rī*, while the two substitutes *alterém* and *alterúī*, endowed with a concurrent characteristic stress shift, performed a distinctly better service as case markers than had done Classical acc. *álteru(m)* or abl. *álterō*. Hence Fr. *autrui*, typically favoured after prepositions (*d'autrui* 'someone else's'), more and more in stereotyped, formulaic sequences; It. *altrui*, qualifying for wider use; OSp. *otrien*; and Ptg. *outrem*.[22] With the rapid weakening of the category of case, through withering of declension, in various Romance languages, the need for contrasting -*ī* and -*em* or -*uī* forms slackened and there occurred instances of mergers that would previously have been unthinkable, as when OSp. *otri (otre)*, through crossing with *otrien*, gave rise to *otrie*, which in turn pushed *nadi* 'nobody', lit. 'a born one' (ie hypercharacterized [*omne*] *nado* 'born man', 'man alive') in the familiar direction of *nadie*. Still, there remained alternative ways, even after the obsolescence of *lo ál*, of keeping apart 'someone else' and 'something else' used as direct objects — by wedging in the preposition *a* between the former and the preceding verb (*veo a otro*) and/or by expanding the latter into more explicit *otra cosa* (cf Fr. *c'est autre chose* side by side with *rien d'autre*, where the use of *rien* insures a modicum of disambiguation).

---

[22] The key role played by *alius/alter* seems unquestionable, but various details elude today's observer. Thus, the split of *aliu-* and *alt(e)ru* must have become wider through the separate developments of -*lj*- and -*l'*-, with the result that *aliorsum* 'elsewhere', marginally preserved in certain daughter languages (Fr. *ailleurs*, Ptg. *alhures*), perished in others (OSp. *ajubre*). The bizarre temporary survival of the by-form *alid*, in lieu of far more common *aliud*, may involve a countermeasure some speakers took to bridge the widening gap, but entailed, in turn, a split, in Old Spanish, between its outgrowth *ál* and *ageno* < *aliēnu*.

Even the near-homonymy of *altus* 'high, deep' may have played a part in these convulsions, witness Rum. *înalt* 'high, tall' (with a prefix plausibly borrowed from a verb, cf Sp. *enaltecer*) beside *alt* 'another, the other'.

Vitally important is the de-emphasis here of the contrast between masculine and feminine, so crucial in other contexts, through tendential generalization of the masculine form. Thus, in those New World dialects of Spanish whose speakers frown on the use of *alguien* and prefer *(alg)uno* instead, females, referring to or including themselves, are apt to have recourse to *uno* rather than to *una*.

We have, with varying degrees of circumstantiality, examined four instances of diachronic hypercharacterization of pronominal gender. True, certain classes of adjectives, to the extent that they interlock with pronouns, have also been involved (as is true of *este, esta*, and the like); from *lo mió . . . lo nuestro* via *lo ál, lo ageno* eventually *lo bueno, lo malo* branched off; the definite articles *(el, la, lo)* also took part in the process at issue; but the pronouns at all times remained at the centre of events. There were interplays between final vowels and stem vowels, especially in Portuguese, and independent interplays, within the former category, between front vowels and back vowels. The feminine was rarely the beneficiary of hypercharacterization (one rare instance was the opening of *e* in Ptg. *esta, essa*, from Lat. *ĭsta, ĭpsa*). The masculine and the neuter, on the other hand, were frequently polarized (OSp. *otri* vs *otra cosa* or *lo ál*; Ptg. *todo* vs *tudo*; Sp. *el* vs *lo*).

With the hypercharacterization of nominal and pronominal gender now under reasonably firm control, the same investigative method of reasoning can be brought to bear on the sharpened marking, across time, of other morphological categories, such as case and number.

References

Alonso 1943. Dámaso Alonso, 'Etimología hispánica, 3: *hasta sa(g)ora*', *Revista de Filología Española* 27 (1943), 30–47.

Appel 1915. C. Appel, *Bernart von Ventadorn: Seine Lieder, mit Einleitung und Glossar* (Halle: Niemeyer, 1915).

Carré Alvarellos 1933. L. Carré Alvarellos, *Diccionario galego-castelán e vocabulario castelán-galego*, 2nd edn (A Cruña [= La Coruña]: Zincke Hermanos, 1933).

Cavacas 1920. A. d'Almeida Cavacas, *A Língua Portuguesa e a sua Metafonia* (Coimbra, 1920).

Cornu 1888. J. Cornu, 'Die portugiesische Sprache', *Grundriss der romanischen Philologie* (ed G. Gröber), 1 (Strassburg: Karl J. Trübner, 1888), 715–803. 2nd edn (1904–06), 916–1037.

Crespo Pozo 1963. J. S. Crespo Pozo, *Contribución a un vocabulario castellano-gallego* (Madrid: Revista 'Estudios', 1963).

Crews 1935. Cynthia M. Crews, *Recherches sur le judéo-espagnol dans les pays balkaniques* (Paris: Droz, 1935).

Dunn 1928–30. J. Dunn, *A Grammar of the Portuguese language* (London: David Nutt [A. G. Berry], 1928–30, for the Hispanic Society of America).

García de Diego. V. García de Diego, *Elementos de gramática histórica gallega. Fonética-morfología* (Burgos: Hijos de Santiago Rodríguez, n.d. [1908]).

Gili 1967. J. Gili, *Catalan Grammar*. Rev 3rd edn (Oxford: The Dolphin Book Co, 1967).

Gulsoy 1969. J. Gulsoy, 'The -*i* words in the poems of Gonzalo de Berceo', *Romance Philology* 23 (1969), 172–87.

Henríquez Ureña 1939. P. Henríquez Ureña, 'Ello', *Revista de Filología Hispánica* 1 (1939), 209–29.

Henríquez Ureña 1940. Id., *El español en Santo Domingo*. Biblioteca de dialectología hispanoamericana 5 (dir A. Alonso) (Buenos Aires: Instituto de Filología, 1940).

Huber 1933. J. Huber, *Altportugiesisches Elementarbuch* (Heidelberg: Carl Winter, 1933).

Keniston 1937. Hayward Keniston, *The syntax of Castilian prose. The sixteenth century* (Chicago: Univ of Chicago Press, 1937).

Lang 1894. H. R. Lang, *Das Liederbuch des Königs Denis von Portugal* (Halle: Niemeyer, 1894).

Lapa 1936. M. Rodrigues Lapa. Review of Huber 1933, *Revista Lusitana* 34 (1936), 301–14.

Lapesa 1948. Rafael Lapesa, 'Asturiano y provenzal en el fuero de Avilés', *Acta Salmanticensia* 2:4, Universidad de Salamanca, 1948.

Leite de Vasconcelos 1907. J. Leite de Vasconcelos, *Textos Arcaicos* (Lisbon: A. M. Teixeira, 1907).

Leite de Vasconcelos 1911. Id., *Lições de Filologia Portuguesa* (Lisbon, 1911). Rev 2nd edn, Lisbon: Biblioteca Nacional, 1926. Rev 3rd edn, Rio de Janeiro: Livros de Portugal, 1959.

Malkiel 1945. Yakov Malkiel, 'Old Spanish *nadi(e), otri(e)*' *Hispanic Review* 13 (1945), 204–30.

Malkiel 1948. Id., 'Hispanic *algu(i)en* and related formations. A study in the stratification of the Romance lexicon in the Iberian peninsula', *Univ. of California Publ. in Linguistics* 1:9 (1948), 357–442.

Malkiel 1957–58. Id., 'Diachronic Hypercharacterization in Romance', *Archivum Linguisticum* 9 (1957), 79–113; 10 (1958), 1–36.

Malkiel 1970. Id., *Linguistica generale, filologia romanza, etimologia* (Florence: Sansoni, 1970).

Malkiel 1973. Id., 'Deux frontières entre la phonologie et la morphologie en diachronie', *Langages* 32 *(Le changement linguistique)* (1973), 79–87.

Malkiel 1977. Id., 'From Phonosymbolism to Morphosymbolism', *The Fourth Lacus Forum*, 511–29.

Malkiel 1979. Id., 'Problems in the diachronic differentiation of near-homophones', *Language* 55 (1979), 1–36.

Menéndez Pidal 1941. R. Menéndez Pidal, *Manual de gramática histórica española*. 6th edn (Madrid: Espasa-Calpe, 1941).

Meyer-Lübke 1890. W. Meyer-Lübke, *Grammatik der romanischen Sprachen*, 1: *Lautlehre* (Leipzig: Fues (R. Reisland), 1890).

Meyer-Lübke 1913. Id., *Historische Grammatik der französischen Sprache*, 1: *Laut- und Flexionslehre*. 2nd and 3rd edns (Heidelberg: Carl Winter, 1913).

Michaëlis de Vasconcelos 1920. Carolina Michaëlis de Vasconcelos, 'Glossário do "Cancioneiro da Ajuda"', *Revista Lusitana* 23 (1920), 1–95.

YAKOV MALKIEL

107

Nunes 1919. J. J. Nunes, *Compêndio de gramática histórica portuguesa: Fonética-morfologia* (Lisbon: A. M. Teixeira, 1919).

Reinhardstoettner 1878. K. von Reinhardstoettner, *Grammatik der portugiesischen Sprache auf Grundlage des Lateinischen und der romanischen Sprachvergleichung bearbeitet* (Strassburg and London: Karl J. Trübner, 1878).

Rohlfs 1949–54. G. Rohlfs, *Historische Grammatik der italienischen Sprache und ihrer Mundarten*. 3 vols, consecutively paged and paragraphed (Berne: Francke, 1949–54).

Schultz-Gora 1911. O. Schultz-Gora, *Altprovenzalisches Elementarbuch* (Heidelberg: Carl Winter, 1911).

Tilander 1937. Gunnar Tilander, 'La terminación -*i* por -*e* en los poemas de Gonzalo de Berceo', *Revista de Filología Española* 29 No. 1 (1937), 1–10.

Williams 1938. Edwin B. Williams, *From Latin to Portuguese; historical phonology and morphology of the Portuguese language* (Philadelphia: Univ of Pennsylvania Press, 1938). 2nd edn 1962, 1968.

Schéma, Sémantique et Pédagogie

GEORGES MATORÉ

Professeur à l'Université de Paris-Sorbonne

Parmi les critiques qui ont été adressées à la pédagogie du français pratiquée dans les enseignements du Premier et Second Degré, l'une, particulièrement justifiée, porte sur l'enseignement du vocabulaire.

Cet enseignement en raison de causes diverses, dues notamment à l'impréparation de certains jeunes maîtres du Primaire, mais aussi à un mauvais aménagement des programmes, s'est dégradé depuis l'entre-deux-guerres. Si l'on compare (certains documents permettent de s'en rendre compte) le vocabulaire de deux enfants de 12 ans du même milieu social en 1935 et en 1979, on constate un appauvrissement caractérisé. Il en serait de même si l'on pratiquait des recherches analogues sur le vocabulaire de lycéens de troisième et sur celui d'étudiants de première année d'Université. Parmi ceux-ci, tel ignore complètement le sens de mots comme *inflation, oléoduc, pragmatisme, euthanasie, conjoncture, collusion* (confondu avec *collision*), etc, ce qui n'empêche nullement le même étudiant d'utiliser parfois des termes techniques ou pédants dont la signification reste pour lui fumeuse. Le mal est connu. Existe-t-il une thérapeutique?

Les moyens employés autrefois étaient discutables. Je me souviens d'avoir eu parmi mes livres de classe, dans ma lointaine enfance, un recueil composé de listes de mots destinés à enrichir le vocabulaire des élèves de l'Enseignement Primaire. Il s'appelait du nom de son auteur, le *Pautex*. Il faut dire que notre instituteur, qui était intelligent, se servait de ces mots nouveaux pour nous aider à confectionner des phrases utiles; le commentaire du mot *étagère* consistait par exemple à bâtir la phrase: 'Jacques monta sur une chaise et rangea ses livres sur le rayon supérieur de l'étagère.' Ces procédés empiriques étaient efficaces quand ils étaient pratiqués avec discernement. Il ne s'agit pourtant pas d'y revenir. Les recueils de mots, qu'ils soient latins, français ou espagnols, ne sont que des nomenclatures isolées de la réalité linguistique.

Les projets de réforme de l'enseignement du français, tels qu'ils ont été proposés il y a quelques années par une trop fameuse 'Commission' ont inquiété tous ceux qui avaient conscience des problèmes concrets que pose la pédagogie et qui se défiaient à juste titre des a priori (non dépourvus d'arrière-pensées) issus d'une psychologie incertaine ou proposés par des linguistiques entre lesquelles aucun accord n'a été conclu. Une chose est d'avancer des théories, autre chose est de promouvoir une pratique efficace. Qu'on se souvienne des méfaits de la lecture globale qui, mal appliquée, nous a légué une génération incapable de maîtriser l'orthographe! On nous a rebattu les oreilles avec la 'créativité', avec la 'nocivité' de la *mémoire* et avec le danger que présente le recours à une norme considérée comme un des auxiliaires les plus précieux de la société de consommation. Soyons sérieux. Veut-on faire de la France une nation qui comprendrait 53 millions de poètes, tous géniaux puisqu'ils se seraient développés sans la contrainte d'une syntaxe rigide et sans les frustrations qu'impose un vocabulaire auquel nombre de cuistres, de Descartes à Montherlant, ont communiqué une pathologique précision?

En attendant qu'on 'brûle l'école' comme le réclamait un des plus chauds partisans de la créativité, il conviendrait d'aviser aux moyens dont nous disposons pour remédier aux déficiences de la pédagogie actuellement pratiquée.

Le vocabulaire constituant un élément beaucoup plus mobile que les sons et la syntaxe, il importe de pratiquer une pédagogie ouverte sur les innovations qu'imposent le mouvement des idées, le développement des techniques, etc. Cela n'implique pas qu'il faille rompre avec le passé. La notion de *norme* ne devra pas être abandonnée, mais on lui communiquera une certaine souplesse; elle restera fondée sur la langue *écrite* et *élaborée* de notre temps qu'il ne faut confondre ni avec un parler académique ni avec le langage familier que l'élève acquerra sans aucune difficulté en dehors de l'école. Une des tâches essentielles du maître, surtout s'il s'adresse à des enfants d'un milieu socio-culturel modeste, est de leur faire saisir l'existence de *niveaux de langue* qui jouent en français, qu'on le regrette ou non, un rôle considérable. Ce n'est pas en développant la créativité qu'on apprendra aux enfants de telle école de banlieue que des mots comme *baffe*, *pompes*, *boulot* et *emmerdant* appartiennent à des parlers marginaux que l'enseignement doit ignorer. Rien n'est moins démo-cratique que de priver des enfants de connaissances 'linguistiques' leur permettant de parler avec 'correction' et, éventuellement, de s'élever dans la vie au-dessus de la condition où risque de les cantonner une langue pauvre et inadéquate. On parle souvent à notre époque d''aliénation'; il n'en est pas de plus grave que celle qui est déterminée par le langage.

Les réformateurs dont il a été fait mention proposaient d'utiliser les 'apports' de la linguistique structurale, ce qui ne signifie rien. Que tous les linguistes d'aujourd'hui soient structuralistes (ou presque) n'implique pas qu'ils ne professent des conceptions très différentes de la structure ni qu'ils aient adopté un vocabulaire homogène. Personnellement je ne vois pas le profit intellectuel que pourraient retirer des élèves à s'inspirer des *analyses componentielles* où se trouvent gravement confrontés le *taureau*, la *vache* et le *veau* (pourquoi pas le *bœuf?*), le *coq*, la *poule* et le *poussin* (et le *poulet?*), l'*homme*, la *femme* et l'*enfant*, etc.

Sans m'attarder ici sur les défauts des pratiques proposées et sans épiloguer sur l'absence de méthode qui est la règle la plus générale et qui ne se justifierait que si l'élève se livrait à des lectures systématiques, je proposerai ici, d'une manière pragmatique, l'utilisation des champs sémantiques.

Bien que subodorée par Saussure sous la forme erronée de 'rapports associatifs' (où se mêlent indûment des associations morphologiques et des analogies de signifiés du type *enseignement* et *instruction*), bien que réalisée d'une manière contestable par les *Sprachfelder* de la sémantique allemande de 1925, bien que poursuivie de nos jours par un certain nombre de lexicologues, dont l'auteur de ces lignes, la sémantique des champs, accusée de *mentalisme* par les structuralistes de stricte obédience, n'a pas suscité l'intérêt qu'on était en droit d'espérer. Ce n'est pas ici le lieu de s'insurger contre la déshumanisation des sciences humaines en général et de la linguistique en particulier qui s'opère sous nos yeux depuis vingt ou trente ans. Quels que soient ses défauts ou ses mérites, la méthode des champs fondée sur la hiérarchie sociologique ou psychologique des faits de vocabulaire semble pouvoir être utilisée aussi bien pour l'acquisition du lexique (enfants, étrangers), que pour illustrer à un niveau scientifique les relations qu'entretiennent les éléments d'apparence parfois hétérogènes constituant une structure lexicologique.

L'intérêt pédagogique de cette méthode provient à mes yeux du fait qu'elle se présente notamment sous la forme visuelle de *schémas.*

Il peut sembler étonnant que notre époque, que René Huyghe définit comme une 'civilisation de l'image', ait fort peu utilisé le schéma dans l'étude des phénomènes linguistiques et littéraires, alors que les historiens par exemple ne se privent pas d'un procédé d'exposition efficace. Appliquée au vocabulaire la pratique du schéma a le mérite, contrairement aux analyses évoquées précédemment, de ne pas se limiter à l'examen de quelques données simples (termes de parenté, couleurs, animaux domestiques, etc), mais de pouvoir s'appliquer à n'importe quel domaine de la vie ou de la pensée. Il est possible (je l'ai fait) de faire figurer dans un schéma les termes qui gravitent autour du mot *religion* au XIIIᵉ siècle, il est également possible de visualiser sous forme d'un tableau les mots relatifs à l'*intelligence (raison, intuition, création, intellectualité,* etc) dans le vocabulaire contemporain.

La méthode proposée présente assurément des difficultés pour le pédagogue qui l'emploiera. Sauf le cas de notions comme *chien* dont la structure est aisée à reconstituer et à laquelle l'élève peut aisément collaborer, l'établissement de *champs* nécessite, pour être mené à bien, des recherches parfois délicates, faisant appel à une documentation sérieuse.[1] Il est évident que le schéma doit être établi avec soin. On s'efforcera autant que possible de marquer les associations que nouent entre eux les mots figurant dans la structure représentée. On indiquera par exemple sur une même horizontale les thèmes apparentés, la verticalité introduisant la notion de hiérarchie. D'autre part, tout schéma doit sauvegarder la lisibilité, or celle-ci interdit à la représentation graphique d'être exhaustive. Il s'agit donc d'établir une sorte de 'cote mal taillée': c'est là une affaire de tact. Le schéma que j'ai établi pour indiquer

---

[1] Qu'il me soit permis de mentionner les deux schémas figurant le champ sémantique du mot *art* (en 1765 et en 1827) que j'ai établis dans une étude faisant suite à la *Méthode en lexicologie* (2ᵉ éd, Paris: Didier, 1974).

graphiquement les thèmes, les mots-clés et les personnages de la *Recherche du temps perdu*[2] a le défaut, que je n'ai pu éviter, d'offrir un nombre trop considérable d'informations.

Je me limiterai ici à l'établissement de trois schémas appartenant à des catégories très différentes: ceux de *chien*, d'*espace* et de *schéma* que je ne présente que comme des esquisses qu'il est sans doute possible de perfectionner. Ces schémas se passent de commentaires. Je suis néanmoins tout disposé à engager un dialogue avec les sémanticiens qui présenteraient des remarques ou formuleraient des objections. J'avais eu l'occasion d'entretenir de ce problème le regretté Ullmann; il s'y était vivement intéressé.

---

[2] G. Matoré et I. Mecz, *Musique et structure romanesque dans la 'Recherche du temps perdu'* (Paris: Klincksieck, 1972).

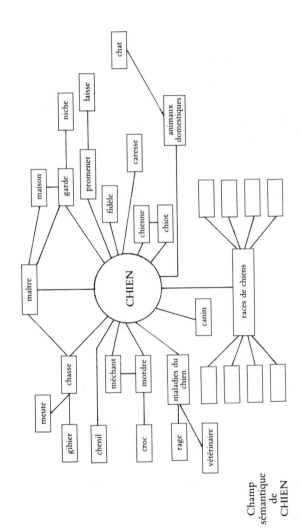

No 1

Champ
sémantique
de
CHIEN

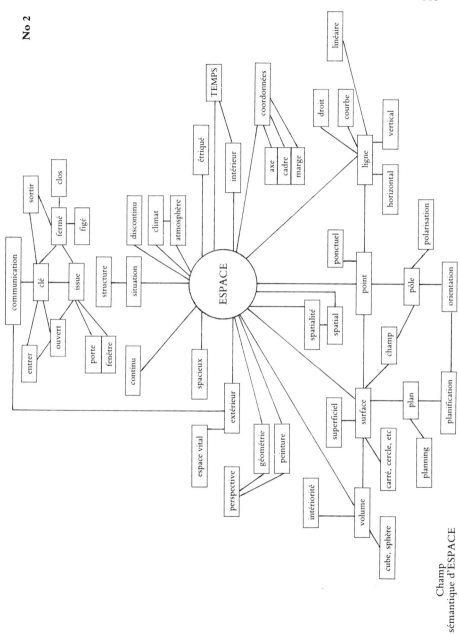

Champ
sémantique d'ESPACE

No 3

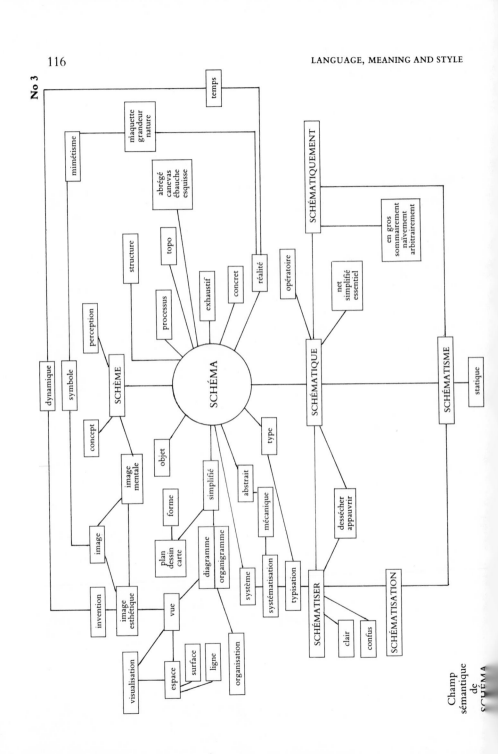

Champ
sémantique
de
SCHÉMA

Lexical gaps and how to plug them

REBECCA POSNER

Professor of the Romance Languages, University of Oxford

Linguistics has been attacked as being more a matter of initiation than of learning, a discipline turned in on itself, more concerned with ideas about language than with the observable data of languages. Indeed it often savours of the *haute blague*, tinkering with theories, of which the principal attraction is their novelty rather than their appropriateness.

The branch of linguistics that is often the least concerned with languages in the plural is semantics, often concentrating on universals rather than particulars, on logic rather than lexicon. It is rare to find semanticists who, like Stephen Ullmann, could combine a consideration of semantic principles with attention to, and practical knowledge of, the lexicon of real languages, including historical and stylistic aspects.

For at the opposite pole to semantics, the most philosophical branch of linguistics, lie lexical studies, frequently the domain of those scholars who abhor generalities and theoretical speculation, who delight in the very diversity of their material and for whom flair and inspiration count more than rigorous method. Moreover, lexical studies are nearly always diachronic in their orientation and philological in their method. Indeed it may be impossible to freeze a lexical synchrony, such is the variation between one individual's vocabulary at different points of time or between different individuals' at the same time. Thus we may wish to relegate lexical studies to a domain outside linguistics proper — perhaps to pragmatics —or to regard the lexicon as the repository of all the irregularities and anomalies that mess up our otherwise elegant linguistic model.

Certainly, for linguists interested only in universals, as many are, lexicon is anathema, for, as any schoolchild knows, languages differ most bewilderingly and unpredictably in the lexical items they use — Frenchmen call cabbages shoes! — and the burden on the memory of learning endless lists of seemingly unstructured items, together with the purely arbitrary constraints on their occurrence, is what makes language learning so hard.

But the amazing thing is that ordinary human beings can store vast numbers (possibly upwards of 50,000) of these items in their long-term memory and can have access to them on the spur of the moment (though speed of access, as well as the size of the store, varies between individuals, and is severely affected by ageing, alcohol or fatigue, as well as by brain lesions). How can we pretend to know anything at all worthwhile about language, when we know so little about how human beings acquire the items, associate them with features of the outside world, remember and recognize them, use them appropriately at the drop of a hat, and also replace them when they go out of fashion?

The complexity of such a storage and retrieval system flabbergasts even those model-builders who are not daunted by syntax.[1] But, in particular, though it can be plausibly claimed that acquisition of grammar is a different process from other learning, the picture looks rather different if we consider vocabulary, for we know that acquisition of vocabulary is intimately linked with learning of skills, that it continues throughout one's lifetime, and that every linguistic community has members who are better speakers than others, usually judged by their richer vocabulary and ability to use graphic and memorable turns of phrase. Moreover we know that changes in lexicon often reflect the material and cultural preoccupations of a society.

So lexical studies will often be spurned by those who want to maintain that language is *sui generis*, the product of an innate human-specific capacity, but not by those who prefer to think of language as a particularly complex sign system.

But how do we link up the universalists' concern with 'meaning' —surely what language is all about — with the lexical study they shun? If we assume, with Roman Jakobson, that 'all cognitive experience is conveyable in any existing language', then we may, as linguists, ask what units of language can convey cognitive experience. Surely the lexeme is one of these units, in spite of Paul Postal's denial of lexeme-sized chunks of meaning. It may be, as Locke maintained, that the lexical unit, when not equivalent to a 'simple idea' (a semantic prime?), is an abbreviation for a 'complex idea' (a

[1] For gropings towards an information retrieval model cf Kenneth I. Forster, 'Assessing the Mental Lexicon', in R. J. Wales and Edward Walker (eds), *New Approaches to Language Mechanisms* (Amsterdam — New York — Oxford: New Holland, 1976), pp 257–87.

semantic configuration?), and even that it can have no precise set of ideas to which it corresponds (a 'fuzzy' concept, or even no concept at all?). But any speaker who uses one lexical item in place of another (like Mrs Malaprop) is subject to ridicule; one who stretches a lexical item beyond acceptable limits (like Humpty-Dumpty) rouses indignation; and one who arbitrarily makes up his own lexical items is either a poet or mad (or both).

Possibly the least interesting way of presenting lexical items is as an unordered list of forms with associated readings and selection restrictions, as in Chomskyan standard theory and ordinary dictionaries (where, to be sure, the artificial alphabetic ordering suits the practical purposes for which they are designed — we recall that the Académie Française originally experimented with more meaningful ordering with no success). Some problems do have to be resolved in this type of presentation: in particular, is there to be a separate entry for every distinguishable reading (homonymy) or only for every phonological form (polysemy)? Can we construct a hierarchy of readings, or are they unordered? and so on. Dictionaries vary in their solutions, often with decisions based ultimately on practical expediency. The Katz-Fodor type of lexicon seems to favour polysemy and hierarchical representation — but the number of actual items presented is tiny, and then the presentation relies heavily on traditional dictionaries. In this essentially semasiological (or interpretive) approach, semantic gaps are not considered. However, with the Halle-Jackendoff type introduction of word-formation rules into the lexicon the question inevitably arises of possible but non-existent morphological derivations — *discussment*, or *blindity*, or *hairful*, for instance. Halle uses a filter device to block their formation, but Jackendoff prefers to leave scope for lexical creativity. Where morphological rules predict a non-existent form, there is a lexical or derivational gap, just waiting to be filled if ever it is wanted.

It is notable that in some cultural contexts many more of these gaps are filled than in others. The sheer exuberance of derivational processes in medieval and Renaissance Romance, in which synonyms were also piled on top of one another, as if by the mere weight of words that will-o'-the-wisp, precise meaning, could be shackled down, contrasts with the sobriety of the Classical periods which sought the *mot juste*, concision and uncluttered elegance. We might make a similar contrast between, for instance, Canadian French, which is tolerant of fanciful derivations, and metropolitan French, in which it has often been claimed that lexical creativity is cribbed, cabined and confined.

Whereas lexicalist semantics favours a polysemic approach to lexical items, generative semantics prefers unconstrained homonymy. As each occurrence of a lexical item is an almost *ad hoc* and arbitrary abbreviation for a semantic configuration, we have difficulty in deciding what are related items. Thus if *règle* must be two items, because we cannot conjoin thus:

Les règles sont strictes et en bois

then so must *ask* because we cannot say (or can we?):

I asked him for £10 and to dinner.

Incidentally, generative semantics is often exemplified by reference to verbs, which are more difficult to define in terms of static semantic components, and which may need to be described more in terms of collocation restrictions than of conceptual attributes.

For generative semantics there must be a virtually limitless number of semantic configurations that remain unlexicalized. For instance:

My basset-hound barks at the postman

is a cognitive experience that has to be strung painfully out over several lexical items — 'articulated' as Martinet would put it — whereas the dog itself may have a single phonological shape, a lexical item, as it were, which denotes only and precisely that. But, of course, he has a limited purview and can reserve an item of his restricted vocabulary for that one experience. Sometimes a seemingly limited experience can be lexicalized in a human language — in Luiseño, for instance, an item *pe?* is glossed 'to eat acorn mush by licking off fingers' (though I hasten to say that, unlike the dog's bark, this can be modified to accommodate different persons and verbal aspects).

However, we need no linguist to tell us that there are many cognitive experiences that we do not lexicalize and that human language is characterized by its ability to break down amorphous experience into linear form. The question then arises, why do we lexicalize anything but 'simple ideas', or 'semantic primes', which must be less numerous and troublesome to store than the lexical items of real languages? Why do we not talk in McCawley-type semantic configurations, or at least in Katz–Fodor semantic features? (We recall that Clark, rather unconvincingly, argued that a young child equates lexical items with single features — perhaps perceptually based — and adds further features later.)[2]

If we did talk only in 'primes', we should presumably be suffering from something akin to amnesic aphasia (though this term is perhaps better reserved for a more deep-seated disorder, with some impairment of abstract attitudes). The well-known mild aphasia experienced by most of us when fatigued can have this effect — though it is usually accompanied by a consciousness of the superficial shape of the word sought. Perhaps we could, by talking only in semantic primes, improve on the scheme worked out by the professors of languages in Balnibarbi (as recounted by Gulliver) — 'for abolishing all words whatsoever . . . a great advantage in point of health as well as brevity'. They, we recall, replaced words with *things* ('since words are only names for things'): unfortunately the women 'in conjunction with the vulgar and illiterate' would have none of it. One disadvantage was that it is too laborious to carry round a sackful of objects, rather than words in one's head.

Similarly, human beings are apparently better at remembering words than at reconstructing anew a whole thought process. Creation is a painful activity, but any reasonably assiduous schoolchild has no difficulty in assimilating and reproducing the ideas that the greatest minds suffered torments to conceive. When cognitive experience is lexicalized it can be neatly stashed away to be taken out and dusted whenever needed.

We can make the far from original hypothesis that lexicalization of a semantic configuration makes it more memorable and economizes that rare commodity, creative effort. Adopting a functionalist standpoint, we can deduce from this premise that semantic configurations that are in frequent use will be readily lexicalized. If we assume also an increase over time in the overall store of knowledge, either of an individual or of mankind in general, we would expect a larger number of semantic configurations to be lexicalized with passage of time, so that lexical (or semantic) gaps would decrease in number.

This seems more or less in accord with our experience, but limiting factors appear to operate, which may result in restriction of the repertoire of

---

[2] Eve V. Clark, 'What's in a word? On the child's acquisition of semantics in his first language', in Timothy E. Moore (ed), *Cognitive Development and the Acquisition of Language* (New York — London: Academic Press, 1973), pp 65–110.

lexical items available, and even in creation of lexical gaps. I shall return to this point.

But generative semantic theory raises another problem. Even if we are to assume that lexicalization of semantic configurations is haphazard, then we still need to distinguish between accidental gaps and systematic gaps. McCawley, discussing what are *possible* lexical items, claims that CAUSE BECOME NOT OBNOXIOUS is not lexicalized in English, whereas CAUSE BECOME NOT ALIVE is (as *kill*).[3] Actually, it has been suggested that both *edify* and *fumigate* could serve here (with the ambiguity of OBNOXIOUS resolved in the lexical item chosen). Whether we accept these as valid mappings or not, it is clear that lexicalization of such a configuration is not impossible, though it may not figure among the most frequently used items of a lexicon.

What then would be an *impossible* lexical item? It may not be a complete waste of time to advance hypotheses on this question, as they are readily falsifiable by adducing examples. Morgan's suggestion that a set of predicates containing an unattached co-ordinator will never be lexicalized seems unobjectionable — like KISS A GORILLA AND (**He flimped an elephant* = 'He kissed a gorilla and an elephant'). One could probably predict (on non-linguistic grounds) that no language, would lexicalize even KISS A GORILLA: but does any lexicalize the more likely KISS A GIRL? Some, of course, would not lexicalize MAKE CONTACT WITH LIPS (*kiss*): English certainly readily lexicalizes configurations part-of-the-body instrumental elements — *kick* (FOOT), *slap* (HAND), *punch* (FIST), *head* (eg a ball), *elbow, knee, eye, nose, finger* — whereas French is comparatively hesitant about such items (but has eg *agenouiller, empoigner*). That it is not unknown to lexicalize a *verb + object* sequence is demonstrated by the Luiseño *pe?* just quoted; French *chevaucher* is another example. Indeed it could be claimed that many apparently intransitive verbs imply (in remote structure) a cognate object: *dream a dream, sleep a sleep, breathe a breath*, etc.

What about subject-verb sequences? Impersonals like *rain* can be analysed as *rain falls*. Can we leave aside items like *bark*, that do no more than presuppose a dog subject in English? Is there any language which expresses such sequences as *the dog barks* with a single item?

---

[3] James D. McCawley, 'On the nature of the "lexical item"', *Chicago Papers in Linguistics*, 4 (1968), pp 71–80.

And how far can modifiers be introduced into the lexicalized configuration? Does any language, I wonder, *lexically* distinguish CAUSE BECOME NOT ALIVE from CAUSE BECOME ALMOST NOT ALIVE?

Negative components could provide an interesting test. In English lexicalization of negatives has greater potential than we often realize. Even practically impossible semantic configurations can be lexicalized — look at the advertisement recently displayed in the London Tube

Make mistakes unhappen

(not = CAUSE NOT OCCUR but CAUSE NOT OCCUR SOMETHING ALREADY OCCURRED, involving a looking-glass world picture). On first reading Manley Hopkins' lines

Margaret, are you grieving
Over golden grove unleaving?

I interpreted the last phrase as NOT *leaving the grove* rather than *the grove losing its leaves* (which would more often be rendered as *unleafing*), but rejected the interpretation as impossible because it seemed to involve two juxtaposed negative components

NOT–NOT STAY *in the grove*

(French *délaisser*, note, is not, as it appears to be, a logical negative of *laisser* but has a negative moral impact 'forsake'.)

One might posit that a sequence of negatives is never lexicalized, but verification would depend on the 'primes' or 'predicates' chosen for the analysis. For instance

CAUSE BECOME NOT–NOT–ALIVE

if we were to follow McCawley, might be lexicalized *revive* or *resuscitate* (depending on real world criteria for not-aliveness). I, however, dislike the NOT-ALIVE interpretation of *dead*, which seems more fundamental (or at least more permanent.) Note, for instance, that transitive forms of *die* verbs can be used for *kill* (like Old French *morir*) and that English has no usual lexical item for

CAUSE BECOME ALIVE

(*animate, enliven* are used figuratively), possibly because in our culture, it is an unusual experience for which the *moyens de fortune* 'bring life to' or 'put life into' will do (though, again, even these are most frequently used figuratively). Note that the more common experience 'give birth', of humans, is not colloquially lexicalized in English (compare the transparent French terms *enfanter, accoucher* with the general words pressed into service in English — *bear, deliver* and even *have* (a baby)), yet *hatch, calve, whelp, farrow, spawn*, etc, proliferate for non-human species.

Is there a language, I wonder, that lexicalizes *unprevent* (NOT-NOT-LET) or *unforbid* (NOT-NOT-ALLOW)? Are not, indeed, *let* and *allow* already lexicalizations of a doubly negative configuration

X NOT DO CAUSE Y NOT DO?

But here the negatives are not juxtaposed and the overall effect is neutral.

Let us consider the interaction of English lexical items that can relate to semantic configurations in this area to see if we can detect lexical gaps. I shall treat STAY (= lack of movement and action) as an inert neutral term: in the appropriate contexts it can be expressed in English as *be left, remain, bide* (which also = *wait* ie stay until a specified point of time, or happening) or *rest*, as well as *stay*. As an extension of the 'lack of movement' meaning *stay* (and also *stop*) can denote more or less permanent residence in a place and also the delaying or prevention of movement. *Stop* is related to *stay* both as a synonym and as an inchoative and a causative: X BEGIN STAY, X CAUSE Y STAY. In the former sense we also find *let up, leave off*, and as an extension of the latter we find 'prevent, hinder' denotations (which, perhaps not quite accidentally, include *let* among their lexicalizations).

These might be termed 'positive' extensions of the neutral STAY. On the 'negative' side we find *let* and *leave* (X NOT DO CAUSE Y NOT STAY) and (X NOT STAY, Y STAY), (X BEGIN NOT STAY), lexical items which interchange in certain contexts and which can be extended to the more emotive 'neglect, abandon, forsake, etc' meanings (X NOT CAUSE Y NOT STAY [in danger, etc]). If we were to posit other possible 'negative' configurations we begin to wander into a no man's land where positive and negative meet: thus X NOT BEGIN NOT STAY might be rendered as *stay* and X NOT DO NOT CAUSE Y NOT STAY could be expressed as *let* (*x lets y be*, etc).

It is to be noted that connection between the 'negative' and the 'positive' side of the schema occurs not only with 'negative' *let* and *leave* being used in the 'positive' expressions *let up* and *leave off*, and in archaic *let* (*without let or hindrance, let ball*), but also in older English uses of *leave*, until the sixteenth century equivalent to *stay*, including the CAUSE TO STAY denotation, and with the French borrowing *remain* which seems originally to have been equivalent to *be left*, but acquired the neutral STAY

meaning that previously *leave* had. *Rest* seems originally to have meant
STAY, acquiring 'repose' connotations when used of animates (while the
noun *rest* also came to be used of 'what is left, a remainder').

Here the interchange between the more frequently used lexical items
suggests a contamination at the lexical level that reflects speakers' fuzziness
about the distinction between the concepts expressed, even to the extent of
confusing 'negative' with 'positive' terms. It is hard to believe that there
have ever been any significant lexical 'gaps' in this rather nondescript
semantic area, though new items have been introduced in the course of
history: besides the borrowings already mentioned, we note that *stop*,
originally referring only to the physical bunging-up, or plugging, of a hole,
was used to supplement *stay* (perhaps because of this word's contamination
with its homonym = 'prop up, *étayer*'). Emotive neologisms are frequent
at both ends of the spectrum — *hinder, fetter, abandon*, etc, but these fill
stylistic gaps rather than semantic ones.

For comparison let us look at the history of some of the popular Romance
words used in similar contexts. (RE)MANERE (= 'stay, remain behind,
continue, endure') has persisted virtually everywhere: in French it was
rivalled by RESTARE ('stand behind, stand still, be left') from the late twelfth
century and was ousted by the seventeenth century. Italian retains both
words: here and there both acquired causative meaning (which is more
characteristic of the derivative ARRESTARE). Other 'lack of movement' verbs
also came to be used in this 'neutral slot': MORARI = 'to linger' persisted as
Span. Port. *morar*, French *demeurer*; *QUIETARE (cf Italian *quietare* = 'soothe')
survives as Spanish *quedar* = 'stay', but also as 'positive' *quitar* = 'prevent'
(cf French 'negative' *quitter* = 'leave', also, like the Spanish word, = 'take
away'); CESSARE = 'delay, loiter, be idle', took on mainly inchoative
meaning in Romance. 'Making firm, getting ready' words also came into
play: *FIGICARE from FIGERE seems to be at the base of Portuguese *ficar*,
FIRMARE (which gives French *fermer* = 'to close') becomes the usual Italian
word for 'to stop' (with the reflexive translated as 'stay' in some contexts);
the Spanish *parar* continues PARARE = 'get ready, arrange', and is cognate
with French *parer* 'to ward off', Italian *parare* 'adorn, shield, keep off, ward
off, block, stop, defend'.

On the negative side RELINQUERE = 'leave behind, remain, neglect', and
PERMITTERE = 'let loose, leave, surrender' persist mainly as Latinisms (but
the range of meanings in the Gallo-Romance area of RELINQUERE is to be

noted — 'forsake, betray, fall down from weakness, abandon nest (of a bird), become detached (of the sole of a shoe)', etc). LAXARE = 'make wide or roomy, undo, slacken' was obviously more popular and gives the most usual words for 'let, leave': Rumanian *a lăsa*, French *laisser* (also *délaisser*, *lâcher*), Italian *lasciare* (also *tralasciare*), Spanish *dejar* (which, interestingly enough, is also a barbarism for *quedar*).

Again, in Romance there is no hint of lexical gap — yet innovations are numerous, possibly more so for 'change of state' verbs than for neutral ones. Emotive neologisms are frequent — for the 'negative' set of meanings of the 'forsake' type, French, for instance, has *abandonner*, *lâcher*, *délaisser* and familiar *plaquer*, *planter*.

I seem to have wandered rather far from my point: in looking for possible systematic lexical gaps, I have strayed into what looks like a familiar 'lexical field' with neutral terms spreading themselves into neighbouring semantic areas and emotively charged semantic configurations abundantly lexicalized by near-synonyms.

What I think emerges is that although a generative semantic approach should lend itself to the study of lexical gaps (whether accidental or systematic), empirically testable hypotheses are impossible without general agreement on the character of semantic primes. Semantic field theory of the Pottier type, which recognizes as *semes* only lexicalized semantic distinctions, rather than abstract predicates, can, on the other hand, allow of such a study — but only in those few areas where a matrix of interacting semes can be posited (kinship terms is the most obvious one). Geckeler surveys attempts to identify such gaps in, for instance, the names of domesticated animals or cookery terms.[4] Obviously gaps of this sort (eg that there is no special lexical item for a neutered dog, whereas there is for a neutered horse, ox, sheep) are accidental and depend on extra-linguistic circumstances.

But apart from lexical areas of this sort (which can be termed 'institutionalized' and which certainly include a good number of technical terms) it is difficult to see how it is possible to envisage lexical gaps in a Saussurean-type sign-system theory where *signifiés* have no existence without *signifiants* and where a difference of *signifiant* necessarily implies a difference of *signifié* (ie there is no absolute synonymy). In some versions

[4] Horst Geckeler, 'Le problème des lacunes linguistiques', *Cahiers de lexicologie*, 25 (1974), pp 31–35.

of this theory the relationship between the *signifiant* and the *signifié* is not bi-directional because a single *signifiant* can be mapped on to more than one *signifié* (in polysemy or homonymy — with one or more signs). Heger's adjustment to the Ogden-Richards triangle (which he converts into a hexagon) overcomes this snag by introducing between the *signifié* and the concept (*noeme*) an additional stage, the *sememe* — a collection of noemes, or semes, which may be mapped conjunctively (in polysemy) or disjunctively (in homonymy) on to one *signifié*, which will then retain its one-to-one relationship with the *signifiant* (so that, presumably, there will be in a language as many signs as there are distinctive *signifiants*).

But whatever version of Saussurean theory we adopt, there can be no *signifiés* without *signifiants*, and therefore no lexical (or semantic) gaps — though there can be derivational gaps, like those mentioned before (ie possible *signifiants* that do not exist because in *langue* they are not mapped on to *signifiés*).

Now, Saussurean theory in its classic form cannot envisage change in *langue*, as the repository of shared judgements among members of a linguistic community. Yet we all know that new signs are constantly being introduced into a language: we must assume that they are thrown up in *parole*, or *discours*, and sometimes subsequently incorporated into *langue*, entailing a wholesale replacement of one system by another. In fact, Saussure himself may well have recoiled before the logical consequences of such a theoretical position, as he is reported as believing that the lexical, as distinct from the grammatical and phonological, system is only loosely structured — which hints at loopholes through which new signs might wriggle, without breaking the network.

Discussion of lexical (or semantic) gaps is most frequent in the context of interlanguage comparison (where lexeme-for-lexeme translation is frequently unsatisfactory or even impossible) or with the study of neologisms, especially loan-words, which often are favoured precisely because speakers are striving for lexeme-for-lexeme translation. For a Saussurean the adoption of a new lexical item (the outward shape of a *signifiant*) must mean the concomitant adoption of a new *signifié* (the linguistic form of a concept). Therefore in a sense there must have previously been a potential *signifié* that lacked a *signifiant* — a lexical gap. In this sense, then, Saussureans must assume that the introduction of a new item into the language must be a response to a need to fill a lexical gap. The dilemma is that, as we have seen, Saussurean theory appears to leave no scope for lexical gaps.

Other difficulties arise: for instance, how do we handle 'lexical swap', in which a single *signifié* is apparently mapped on to different *signifiants* at different times? Coseriu suggests that Old French *ocire* and modern *tuer* have identical *signifiés*, but that one *signifiant* has been substituted for the other (thus there has been no semantic change).[5] Of course, there was a long transitional period in which both *ocire* and *tuer* were used: it might be claimed by a classical Saussurean that the different *signifiants* were matched by different *signifiés* during this period, with subsequent loss of one of the *signifiants* and amalgamation of the *signifiés*:

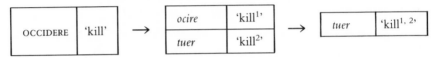

But Coseriu would presumably claim that *ocire* and *tuer* were never elements of the same 'functional' language, but that the 'historical' language in which they co-occurred would embrace the two 'functional' languages that contained them as translation equivalents. The 'lexical swap' would be a result of borrowing from one functional language to the other, and concomitant loss of the *ocire* item.

Coseriu distinguishes such 'lexical swap' from 'semantic change', which, he insists, concerns only shifts in *signifiés* (manifested, of course, by concomitant *signifiant* changes). The example he gives:

VETUS	*viejo*
VETULUS	

suggests an amalgamation of *signifiés* and thus lexical loss. Such loss suggests that in some sense a lexical gap is created: in Coseriu's example, the distinction [± human] is no longer marked as a lexical contextual feature. In some cases real-life confusion can be caused by lexical loss:

[5] Eugenio Coseriu, 'Pour une sémantique diachronique structurale', *Travaux de Linguistique et de Littérature publiés par le Centre de Philologie et de Littérature romanes de l'Université de Strasbourg*, 2 (1964), pp 139–86.

touaille	
serviette	serviette
portefeuille	portefeuille

where *serviette* has come to designate not only 'towel' and 'table napkin', but also 'brief-case'.

To take another example, cited by Benveniste: *menuisier* — originally designating someone who did any delicate work (whittling down things) — now is used only for a 'joiner', leaving a lexical gap which is left unfilled, while *menuisier* is not generally connected by speakers with the verb *amenuiser* (= 'to make smaller').[6]

But introduction of a new item can fill a previously unfelt gap. English *cheat*, for instance, originally referred to Norman lords' confiscation of what they felt was due to them (from *échoir*); *trick* was adopted in the sixteenth century from no one knows where, while *swindle* was a later German borrowing; *hoax*, *humbug*, *fool*, *hoodwink*, *bamboozle*, *cozen* were all introduced at late stages. Old English *wrench* survives only in its (original?) physical sense, whereas *blench* has disappeared from the standard language in the 'trick' sense. Another 'witchcraft' word *wile*, and its Frenchified form *(be)guile*, have survived better, but with such anodyne connotations that they could not stem the flood of innovations.

In French, similarly, innovations are numerous: the most usual word today is *tromper*, introduced in the fourteenth century, probably as an echo of the fairground (= 'to blow trumpets'), and rivalled by *tricher*, probably of dialectal origin, but which tended to specialize in the 'cheat (at cards etc)' sense, from the seventeenth century. *Décevoir*, echoing DECIPERE, was less vivid and took over the rôle of *désappointer* (already archaic by the time of the 1718 Académie dictionary); *guil(l)er* had died out by the seventeenth century (surviving in dialects with a variety of specialized meanings); *enganer* and *engignier* likewise died out. *Duper* recalls the supposed gullibility of the hoopoe (similar to English *gull*); FRAUDARE, which survived until, and after, Villon as *frouer*, *flouer*, a slang word for *tricher*, is still used today in connection with snaring birds. Modern French slang uses a series of

---

[6] Emile Benveniste, 'Comment s'est formée une différenciation lexicale en français', *Cahiers Ferdinand de Saussure*, 22 (1966), pp 15–28.

colourful synonyms — *carotter, pigeonner, piper, rouler* — of transparent metaphoric content.

It is easy to deduce from these examples that it is not the presence of a lexical gap that prompts the coining of new terms, but a desire for innovation. Romance languages other than French have continued to prefer *INGANARE words that seem to have been coined at a common Romance stage (cf *deganare* = *inludere* in the Reichenau glosses), though Rumanian apparently borrowed *înșela* from the Slavs. Spanish introduced alongside *engañar* such words as *estafar* (from Italian *staffare* = 'to get one's foot caught in a stirrup'), *timar* (a slang word of uncertain origin) and the Latinism *defraudar*, while Italian coined *barare* (apparently formed from *barone* — cf English *cheat*) and *raggirare* (from *girare*) alongside *ingannare*.

A doctrinaire position that denies the possibility of synonymy could maintain that such neologisms fill lexical gaps, but it seems more reasonable to assume that they merely refine and animate an area already comfortably, if unexcitingly, covered by the most frequently used items.

The introduction of a neologism then is no evidence for the existence of a lexical gap — though, of course, newly discovered or invented objects sometimes prompt lexicalization. But even here, if we apply the Minimax Principle enunciated by Carroll and Tanenhaus[7] we anticipate that speakers will fill such obvious gaps most readily by using an already familiar term (*imposture lexicale*, as Polge called it),[8] as when a 'pin', the pointed object we use for fastening papers and so on together, was given the same name in English as was used for a 'feather', 'peg' or 'pen', or, in French, as was used for a 'thorn'). This is what I have called the thingummybob principle, often involving extension of designation on formal or functional grounds. Almost as often, a combination or derivation based on already familiar items will be used — like *pomme de terre* or *love apple* with true neologisms like *potato* and *tomato* less readily adopted by standard usage. Even when a new term is launched with the product, speakers may drift back to an old one: thus *automobile*, as a noun, fades before *car, voiture, macchina, coche, carro*.

[7] J. M. Carroll and M. K. Tanenhaus, 'Prolegomena to a functional theory of word-formation', *Chicago Linguistic Society Parasession on Functionalism* (1975), pp 47–62.

[8] Henri Polge, 'En marge de l'Atlas Linguistique de la Gascogne. L'innovation lexicale et son conditionnement', *Via Domitia*, 17 (1962), pp 51–62.

However, the introduction of new words for new objects is the most easily exemplified way of filling lexical gaps. Most examples cited are substantives: let me illustrate with the names for a new process — knitting, which was introduced into Europe by the Arabs, via Spain. For us the process seems to merit a special name — though English *knit* is etymologically related to *knot* and we are not always clear about the semantics of *knitting one's brow*. In French, too, *tricoter* is a pretty specific lexicalization, though a fairly recent one: only last century there was still confusion about the relationship of *tricoter* = 'to move something quickly' and the click-clack of needles; Sensine describes a cartoon depicting a young girl dancing (*qui tricote les jambes*) ageing to an old crone knitting (*qui tricote*).[9] Perhaps the decisive factor in the adoption of the lexicalization was the use, since the seventeenth century, of the place name *Tricot* for a cloth manufactured there. Spanish does not lexicalize the action but uses a periphrase *hacer punto de media*, while Italian uses, besides similar *fare la calza*, *lavorare a maglia*, in which *maglia* is apparently borrowed from French *maille* = 'a link in chain mail or a net', by metaphoric transfer from the Latin word for a 'spot, stain' MACULA which continued as Italian *macchia* (French adopted the (Frankish?) word *tache* in this sense). Rumanian has borrowed *tricota* from French for the process, but also uses the more common and general 'weaving and plaiting' word *împleti*.

How sober and economical the languages are about knitting, which does not always rate a lexical item of its own, and yet how exuberant they are about cheating and tricking! It seems that against the *thingummybob* principle is working a 'Caution to the Winds' syndrome with speakers relishing the very sound of the words they use. Poetry and word-play form the realm of lexical creativity: users rejoice in pro-liferating words and in making bold transfers of sense. But classical good taste and scientific discourse try to impose on slangy vulgarity the tidy *mot juste* principle — a word for everything and every word in its place. In different languages, or at different stages of the same language, one or other of the conflicting principles may prevail, but the conflict may always be there. In pseudo-psychological terms, *thingummybob* is

[9] Henri Sensine, *Nécrologie verbale: études sur le passé et le présent de la langue française* (Lausanne: Payot, 1933).

schizoid,[10] 'Caution to the Winds', hysteric, and *mot juste*, obsessive compulsive.

Am I therefore saying that lexical gaps are a figment of the imagination, an artifact of defective lexical theory, or a fixation of the obsessive compulsive personality?

Perhaps so. What is certain is that linguistics has not yet advanced a viable theory of neologism, which would form part of a more general theory of lexical structure. We look to psycholinguistics and neurolinguistics to provide information about acquisition and disintegration of vocabulary and word-meanings, but unfortunately, so far, there seems to be no consensus of opinion. Do children first acquire terms for concrete things and then generalize,[11] do they proceed from semantic primes,[12] or do they first comment on dynamic relationships, only later identifying static attributes?[13] The progress of vocabulary from the ten or so 'words' a child uses at fifteen months to the 5000 or so he might 'know' at entry to school is still obscure — perhaps because psycholinguists pay more attention to development of 'concepts' than to the linguistic units that relate to them.

Neurolinguists, too, are uncertain about how far aphasia, in its various forms, stems from purely linguistic disorders or from deeper intellectual disorders.[14] One might hope to gain from studies of verbal aphasia and paraphasia some insight into the way vocabulary is stored and accessed: however such studies of necessity are concerned with individuals and may only obliquely cast light on the problems of lexical history, which concern the shared lexicon of a linguistic community rather than the idiosyncrasies of an individual's vocabulary.

Instead of a broadly onomasiological approach to lexicon — considering what might be and is expressed in terms of lexical units — a purely semasiological approach is possible. Let me throw out a hypothesis which in a remote way reflects what Dixon tells us happens in the Australian language Dyirbal, where a reduced lexicon, used in the hearing of taboo

[10] For the failure of schizophrenics to distinguish homonyms, cf L. Irigaray, *Le langage des déments* (The Hague: Mouton, 1973).
[11] Jeremy M. Anglin, *The Growth of Word-Meanings* (Cambridge, Mass: MIT Press, 1970).
[12] Eve V. Clark, *op. cit.*
[13] Katherine Nelson, 'Concept, Word and Sentence: inter-relations in acquisition and development', *Psychological Review*, 81 (1974), pp 267–85.
[14] Macdonald Critchley, *Aphasiology* (London: Arnold, 1970).

relatives, can be translated into normal speech with the use of more specific vocabulary.[15] The lexicon of a language — or perhaps more properly the vocabulary of an individual — has a framework, not of abstract semantic primes, nor indeed of more complex concepts, but of actual lexical items, learned perhaps early in life, and covering fairly adequately, but unspecifically, much of cognitive experience. This lexicon is expanded not by 'plugging gaps' so much as by refining the mesh of the network and introducing more delicate nuances or more striking expressions. (This is not however to say that general terms are necessarily more 'basic' than specific ones — for instance, though *tree* is no doubt more 'available' to English speakers than *oak*, *ash*, etc, it seems that *dog* is learned earlier, and is more readily available, than *animal*, no doubt for cultural reasons.)

One would expect the 'basic' lexicon to remain fairly stable over time — though lexical swap can obviously occur (to be detected most easily via the loss of items). One might expect, too, that it would cover experience that is, if not actually universal, at least not specific to a single community. One would also expect the basic items to occur relatively frequently in discourse. But how many and which?

Certainly there must be some limit to the number of items in the repertoire — otherwise why should items ever be lost? I have maintained elsewhere that lexical loss is the key to many of the problems of historical semantics.[16] Some languages at some conjunctures are all too ready to reject their old words: late seventeenth-century polite French society — obsessive compulsive if ever a community was — is the best illustration I know of the *mot juste* principle taken to extremes, with the curious consequence that it operated with an almost pathologically restricted lexicon (but that was because it regarded so many things as unspeakable). Other communities seem to go on hoarding words — Spanish is an extreme example, but English comes a good second. But the number of words listed as available in a current dictionary is no guide to the size of vocabulary speakers actually use (what makes for 'availability' or 'currency' has received little attention).[17] The Stanford Romance Languages project makes the assumption that for practical purposes about 5000 items will cover the vast majority of

---

[15] Richard W. Dixon, *The Dyirbal Language of North Queensland* (Cambridge: CUP, 1972).

[16] Rebecca Posner, 'Homonymy, Polysemy and Semantic Change', *Language Sciences*, 27 (1973), pp 1–8.

[17] But cf, for example, Naum Dimitrijević, *Lexical Availability* (Heidelberg: Groos, 1969).

non-specialized discourse. Verbs like *tricoter* or *tricher* do not figure in this restricted vocabulary: *tromper* does, and must have displaced other items when it came to prominence in the fourteenth century.

Can we perhaps postulate some storage or retrieval constraint that cuts the vocabulary down to size and favours the operation of the *thingummybob* principle? However, when polysemy (or homonymy) threatens to be pathological, Gilliéron's therapeutic reaction sets in and a new means of expression gains favour.

Alongside this, the 'hysterics', intoxicated by the magic of the words themselves, will be introducing new ones (or revivifying old ones). A memory constraint might operate to reduce synonymy by allowing worn-out words to be ousted by attractive new ones. Meanwhile the obsessives toil away at trying unambiguously to fill lexical gaps. Their coinings may attract prestige and enter the general lexicon: thus, for instance, *motivated* replaces *keen* (of students, etc) which then takes its place among the numerous ephemeral slang terms expressing approval.

In order to test these hypotheses we should have to construct a sample 'basic' lexicon — using, perhaps, not only frequency criteria, but other tests for availability (including information culled from children and aphasics). Historical Romance linguistics has a rôle to play here, I believe, for a study of the shared vocabulary of all the Romance languages, comparing also the innovations made by each, may give insight into what items are most resistant to change, and what factors lead to change.

Shades of Swadesh glottochronology, it may be said. In a way, but the Swadesh technique uses lexicon to discover non-lexical information — the degree of relationship between languages — and is purely quantitative, not qualitative. Hence the use of a very short list of lexical items — most usually 100 — which are deemed to be non-culture-specific. It is of course laughable to think that any sane and adult human being could survive normally in society with only one hundred items of vocabulary. But any normal vocabulary must be related to the culture of the community (for example, the Edinburgh adolescents tested by Dimitrijević seem to have as their most 'available' item for foodstuffs *potatoes* — perhaps it is a sign of the times that both *haggis* and *porridge* figure very low on their lists).

An advantage of using comparative Romance information for the construction of a hypothetical 'basic' lexicon is that most Romance-speaking communities have similar cultures, with differences that are readily identifiable. If a comparatively unchanging 'basic' list of items forms the framework of the lexicon of a community, it should be easier to put in perspective the lexical innovations and losses that occur through time.

Thus it may be possible to avoid the triviality that often characterizes studies of the lexicon, without, in our search for a theory, resorting to the sort of onomasiological approach that envisages mythical lexical gaps that have to be plugged.

On Certain Tense-Values in Molière

T. B. W. REID†

Professor Emeritus; formerly Professor of the Romance Languages in the University of Oxford

It seems to be generally assumed that the syntax of literary French, like its morphology, has changed comparatively little since the later seventeenth century; changes there have certainly been in phonology and vocabulary, but the forms of inflected words and the functions associated with those forms, as found, say, in a play of Molière, are widely believed to be familiar and transparent to a twentieth-century hearer or reader. This belief, however, is not always justified as regards either logical values or stylistic overtones. The following notes draw attention to certain instances in which Molière's use of mood, and sometimes also tense, appears to have been misunderstood by some modern critics and editors. They are taken chiefly from *Le Misanthrope*, for which we have a detailed commentary from the pen of a distinguished French scholar of the present century, Gustave Rudler.[1]

Though Rudler would not have claimed to be a historian of the French language, on matters of syntax he does often cite the work, still standard today, of A. Haase;[2] it should be noted, however, that not all such citations are really relevant to the passage under discussion. Thus on the lines

> Et jamais, de son cœur, je n'aurai de pardon,
> Pour n'avoir pas trouvé que son sonnet *fût* bon! (*Mis.* 1515–16),

---

[1] Molière, *Le Misanthrope*, ed Gustave Rudler (Oxford: Blackwell, 1947, reprinted 1952). Quotations from *Le Misanthrope* are given as in this edition, which according to Rudler (p xlii) reproduces the 'texte généralement reçu', with modernized spelling. Quotations from other plays follow the text of the Grands Écrivains edition.

[2] But he uses the first edition of the French translation (A. Haase, *Syntaxe française du XVIIᵉ siècle*, trad M. Obert, Paris, 1898), and nearly always cites the page-number alone, without paragraph-number, so that his references are difficult to trace in the revised edition (1914 and reprints) which is used by most scholars and is cited in the present notes.

he comments: '*fût*: ce subjonctif après un verbe de supposition accompagné d'une négation était usuel. Cf Haase, 195', overlooking the fact that the long discussion in Haase (§ 80) is concerned only with the use of the subjunctive mood in clauses depending on such verbs in *non*-negative contexts, as in 'Je pensois que tout *fût* perdu' (*Mariage forcé*, sc. iv). Haase evidently took it as axiomatic that in the clause depending on a verb of this type used negatively the subjunctive would be normal in the seventeenth century as in his own time;[3] if Rudler finds its use by Molière in need of explanation, one can only assume that he, and no doubt others of his generation, would have been inclined to write 'pour ne pas avoir trouvé que son sonnet était bon'. For him the sense would have been the same, the stylistic value different.

Misunderstanding of the text of Haase is not, however, involved in certain other failures of analysis in the same general field of the syntax of mood, and particularly that of the imperfect subjunctive. Thus on the lines

> Et penserait paraître un homme du commun,
> Si l'on voyait qu'il *fût* de l'avis de quelqu'un (*Mis.* 675–6),

Rudler comments: '*fût*: pour la concordance des temps, et pour signifier qu'il n'en est pas d'avis'. This suggests that he would himself have written not *fût* but *est*. In Molière's French, however, as still in that of many conservative writers today, the subjunctive is obligatory in a noun clause in this situation, simply because it depends on the hypothetical clause *si l'on voyait*. It is true, of course, that the sequence of tenses required for Molière (and still requires today for those who write in the appropriate style) the imperfect and not the present subjunctive; but it is not true that the use of the subjunctive excludes the possibility that Alceste might agree with someone (it is not stated, or implied, 'qu'il n'en est pas d'avis'), though any such agreement is purely hypothetical.

That for Rudler the natural tense to use in a construction of this type was the present indicative rather than the imperfect subjunctive seems to be confirmed by the text as he prints it in *Mis.* 663–4:

> Et son cœur à railler trouverait moins d'appas,
> S'il avait observé qu'on ne l'*applaudit* pas.

---

[3] Cf M. Grevisse, *Le Bon Usage*, 4ᵉ éd, Gembloux and Paris, 1949 (and later eds), § 999 (b); W. von Wartburg and P. Zumthor, *Précis de Syntaxe du français contemporain*, 2ᵉ éd (Berne: Francke, 1958), § 420 (b).

In conversational French of the twentieth century, as far as grammar is concerned, the present indicative might well pass: 'if Célimène had observed that people are not applauding her'. It is true that even if the hypothetical character of *s'il avait observé* failed to evoke the classical subjunctive in the dependent noun clause (where indeed the indicative is far from unusual nowadays), the sequence of tenses would still require the imperfect *applaudissait*: but that requirement too is now sometimes disregarded. The combination of these two derogations, however, is inconceivable in the usage of Molière; what he wrote must have been the imperfect subjunctive *applaudist*,[4] and it is *applaudît* that stands in the Grands Ecrivains and other good modern editions.[5] But it is not only a matter of grammatical principles: the present indicative really makes the sentence meaningless in its context, for Alceste's whole point is precisely that people *do* applaud Célimène's slanders.

Equally misleading are the implications of Rudler's note on *Mis.* 539–40,

> C'est un homme à jamais ne me le pardonner,
> S'il savait que sa vue *eût pu* m'importuner:

'*eût pu* (et non "a pu"), soit pour la concordance des temps, soit pour éloigner l'hypothèse'. Not only is there no question here of two alternative explanations, as suggested by 'soit . . . soit'; if the sentence is to mean what Molière intended, there is no possibility of the use, either in the seventeenth or in the twentieth century, of the perfect indicative *a pu*. As in *Mis.* 676 and 664 discussed above, the subjunctive mood is required by classical syntax in the noun clause depending on a hypothesis (*s'il savait que* . . .); the use of the subjunctive cannot make the fulfilment of the hypothesis any more remote. If, however, the subjunctive had not been imposed by the construction, the verb in the noun clause would still not have been *a pu*, or even, with correct observance of the sequence of tenses, *avait pu*. What Célimène does not wish Acaste to know is not, in direct speech, 'sa vue a pu m'importuner', or, in indirect speech depending on a verb in a past tense, '(il savait que) sa vue avait pu m'importuner': in fact, she has not yet seen Acaste, and therefore cannot have been incommoded

---

[4] Cf the reproduction of the original edition in the Textes Français series (Paris, Les Belles Lettres, 1946).

[5] There are, it is true, other twentieth-century editions (including the Pléiade) that print *applaudit*.

by seeing him. What she actually does not wish him to know is, in direct speech, 'sa vue pourrait m'importuner', in indirect speech '(il savait que) sa vue aurait pu m'importuner'. The pluperfect subjunctive *eût pu* is therefore an instance of the 'subjunctive of the conditional': besides being in the subjunctive mood required by its dependence on *s'il savait que* . . ., it is also what has been called a 'conditionnel passé deuxième forme', equivalent in sense to the normal conditional perfect *aurait pu*.[6] The commoner tense of the 'subjunctive of the conditional', the imperfect, occurs in, eg, *Mis.* 569–70:

> N'a-t-il point quelque ami qui *pût*, sur ses manières,
> D'un charitable avis lui prêter les lumières?

in which the interrogation with *pût* corresponds to an affirmative statement of the form 'Il a un ami qui *pourrait* . . .'. We have the same usage in *Mis.* 1041–4:

> Vous voyez, elle veut que je vous entretienne . . .
> Et jamais tous ses soins ne pouvaient m'offrir rien
> Qui me *fût* plus charmant qu'un pareil entretien.

Here Rudler notes that *pouvaient* is a 'latinisme probable, pour "auraient pu"' (cf Haase § 66 D), but fails to draw the conclusion that *fût* must then represent the subjunctive not of *était* but of *serait*. The 'subjunctive of the conditional', even in the form with the pluperfect subjunctive as in *Mis.* 540, is still in literary use (Grevisse § 1054, 4°), and it is interesting to find an example in Rudler's own introduction to *Le Misanthrope*: '3600 hémistiches, se faisant face et se défiant l'un l'autre, je doute que Molière lui-même les *eût fait* passer' (p xxxix), which would correspond to a positive statement 'je crois que Molière lui-même ne les *aurait* pas *fait* passer'.

The modern critic's uncertainty about the function of the subjunctive mood and the sequence of tenses in classical French is strikingly illustrated by Rudler's comment on *Mis.* 899–902:

> Et je me vis contrainte à demeurer d'accord
> Que l'air dont vous *viviez* vous *faisait* un peu tort,
> Qu'il *prenait* dans le monde une méchante face,
> Qu'il n'*est* conte fâcheux que partout on n'en fasse . . .

---

[6] Cf Grevisse, § 1054, 4°, and most of the examples in Haase, § 67 B.

Here (though in the literary commentary, not in the linguistic notes) he says: '*viviez*, un subjonctif, *faisait*, *prenait*, deux imparfaits, prétendent encore éloigner le blâme. Mais le v. 902 passe au présent: Arsinoé découvre ses crocs: une véritable allure de serpent'. But there is no conceivable justification for taking *viviez* as a subjunctive (in any case, even if the subjunctive mood were possible in this context, the tense would have to be the imperfect *vécussiez*): *viviez* in the relative clause, like *faisait* in the clause on which it depends and *prenait* in the following line, is an imperfect indicative; and these imperfects, in normal sequence on the past tense *vis* of the principal clause, cannot in any way attenuate the expression of censure. It is true, of course, that with the change to the present in line 902 Arsinoé 'bares her teeth', though the nature of the grammatical device is not exactly that suggested by Rudler: she forgets that she is supposed to be reporting a conversation of the previous day in which she had allegedly tried to defend Célimène, and by breaking the sequence of tenses ('je me *vis* contrainte à demeurer d'accord . . . Qu'il n'*est* conte fâcheux . . .') reveals that she is herself condemning her.

It seems probable that Rudler was also mistaken (though here in company with many other critics) about the stylistic implications of certain of Molière's uses of the imperfect subjunctive. On *Mis.* 427–8,

> Je voudrais bien, pour voir, que, de votre manière,
> Vous en *composassiez* sur la même matière,

he comments: '*com-po-sa-ssiez*: on croirait ce ` long mot prononcé syllabe par syllabe, avec un rictus d'ironie féroce'. Here he speaks only of the length of the word; but in attributing comic force to the 'gros adverbe' *in-du-bi-ta-ble-ment* in line 452 he declares that 'il vaut le *com-po-sa-ssiez* d'Oronte'. Now words of four syllables, unlike those of six, are not at all rare in this or other plays of Molière; so if there was for him anything strikingly expressive about *composassiez*, it must have resided not in the mere length of the word but in the imperfect subjunctive ending *-assiez*, a form that has commonly been held up to ridicule in the nineteenth and twentieth centuries. Similar forms in other seventeenth-century texts, used in the same syntactical context (a noun clause depending on a verb of will, necessity, etc, in the conditional mood) have been widely characterized by modern critics as having intrinsic comic force, eg

> Voudriez-vous, faquins, que j'*exposasse* l'embonpoint de mes plumes
> aux inclémences de la saison pluvieuse, et que j'*allasse* imprimer
> mes souliers en boue? (*Préc. rid.*, sc. vii).

On the other hand, Racine, and presumably his contemporary
audience, saw nothing in the least comic about similar forms, occurring
in exactly the same syntactical conditions, in passages in his tragedies
such as:

> Ne voudriez-vous point qu'approuvant sa furie . . .
> Je *suivisse* à l'autel un tyrannique époux,
> Et que dans une main de votre sang fumante
> J'*allasse* mettre, hélas! la main de votre amante? (*Mithr.* IV ii),

or

> Pour bien faire il faudrait que vous le *prévinssiez* (*Andr.* II i).

Stephen Ullmann, drawing attention to the grave danger of pro-
jecting modern stylistic values on to texts of earlier periods,[7] rightly
stresses the significance of differences of register; he points out that forms
which were comic in the farcical prose of the *Précieuses ridicules* need not
have produced the same effect in the verse comedy of *Le Misanthrope*, any
more than in the tragic verse of Racine, and he rejects the usual
interpretation of the *composassiez* of Oronte. It seems probable, however,
that he might have gone even farther. It is difficult to see how any
grammatical form can produce a special effect, in whatever style of speech
or writing, unless it is deliberately chosen in preference to an alternative
form which could have been used in the same context without producing
that effect. Now, was there available to Molière any grammatical
alternative to the imperfect subjunctive in the noun clause depending on a
verb of will in the conditional mood? Could he, in particular, have
substituted the present subjunctive, which is now normal in such contexts
in spoken French? This usage is in fact attested already in the seventeenth
century;[8] it is mentioned by the grammarian Oudin in 1632 as an error made

---

[7] In W. von Wartburg, *Problèmes et méthodes de la linguistique*, 2ᵉ éd, Paris, 1963, pp 226–7
(= *Problems and Methods in Linguistics*, tr J. M. H. Reid (Oxford: Blackwell, 1969), pp 207–8).

[8] It should be stressed that this applies only to clauses depending on a 'form in -*rais*' in the
function of a present conditional (not in that of a future in the past indicative); in clauses
depending on verbs in true past tenses the replacement of the imperfect subjunctive by the
present does not seem to be attested before the nineteenth century.

by speakers belonging to the East of France, and forty years later it begins to appear in familiar letters such as those of Mme de Sévigné.[9] There is no evidence, however, that this 'incorrect' usage was known to Molière. No instance of it has been cited from his plays, in which the tense used in this construction is always the imperfect subjunctive, not only in the speech of courtiers or bourgeois but also in that of servants or peasants, eg

> Je voudrions, Monsieu, que vous nous *baillissiez* quelque petite drôlerie pour la garir (*Méd. malgré lui* III ii);
>
> Où est-ce donc qu'il peut être? — Je ne sai; mais je voudrois qu'il *fût* à tous les guebles (*ib.* III iv).

Nor does it make any difference whether the verb-form in question is an unobtrusive *eût* or *fût* or one of those forms now considered grotesque such as *prisse, épousasse*, etc. In fact, there seems to be no real evidence that any imperfect subjunctive forms, even those in *-assions, -ussiez*, etc, were ever felt to be comic or pedantic or inelegant until about a century later, in the 1770s and '80s.[10] It would therefore appear that in these clauses depending on *je voudrais*, etc, Molière was not aware of having any choice of verb-form. The only possible tense was the imperfect subjunctive; and that tense, whatever its forms, was therefore incapable of carrying any of the overtones of irony or pedantry or parody that have been attributed to it. And this must have been the situation irrespective of register: the *exposasse* and *allasse* of the *Précieuses ridicules* were intrinsically as neutral and colourless as the *composassiez* of *Le Misanthrope* and the *prévinssiez* of *Andromaque*. Stylistically, therefore, the gulf in this respect between the usage of the classical period and that of modern French is indeed enormous.

[9] F. Brunot, *Histoire de la langue française*, III, 2 (Paris, 1911), p 588; IV, 2 (Paris, 1924), p 998.
[10] Brunot, *op. cit.*, VI, 2 (par A. François; Paris, 1933), p 1458.

Historical Semantics and the Structure of Medieval French Vocabulary

WILLIAM ROTHWELL

Professor of French Language and Medieval Literature, University of Manchester

Over twenty years ago Stephen Ullmann saw that the development of structuralist ideas in linguistics had not advanced at a uniform pace in all branches of the discipline and that the area least affected by the new thinking was semantics — in particular, historical semantics. His response to this realization was published in the *Homenaje a André Martinet*[1] under the title 'Historical Semantics and the Structure of the Vocabulary' (pp 289–303), where he sought to demonstrate how structural ideas might be applied to specific sections of the vocabulary of French, viewed in historical perspective. Some years later Eugenio Coseriu took up the idea again in his article 'Pour une sémantique diachronique structurale',[2] noting his predecessor's work and going on to develop, with examples taken in considerable part from medieval French, a detailed argument illustrating the changes in the structural opposition of a number of terms as they passed from Latin to modern French. Both these studies are to be welcomed as important contributions towards freeing historical semantics from the stigma of condescension that so often attaches to it. For, as Professor Posner has recently expressed it in a stimulating article in *Language Sciences*:[3] 'Work in historical semantics is often regarded as naïve and superficial, largely because it easily descends to the anecdotal, rarely seeing the wood of semantic theory for the trees of detailed lexical usage' (p 1). She goes on to develop this criticism: 'What is regarded as particularly unsatisfactory theoretically about most work in historical semantics is that it is irretrievably lexeme-based' (p 1), adding that: 'Investigation of the data that

[1] Buenos Aires, 1956.
[2] *Travaux de Linguistique et de Littérature* II, 1 (1964), pp 139–86.
[3] 'Homonymy, Polysemy and Semantic Change', vol 27 (1973), pp 1–8.

interest historical semanticists requires no very profound semantic theory'
(p 3).[4]

For all these scholars the trouble with historical semantics, then, is that it
tends to concentrate on the alterations of meaning occurring in individual
words through the centuries, thus failing to offer any global view of the
linguistic situation at any particular time and of the underlying processes at
work within it. But the historical semanticist may have something to offer
as well as to learn, as the following examples may show. Since all three
articles use medieval French in order to illustrate their arguments, it may be
useful to look closely at some of the cases they discuss, bringing to bear on
them such evidence as is available from standard works of reference.[5]

Both Stephen Ullmann and Eugenio Coseriu open up new perspectives
in the diachronic study of meaning. The former's proposal to describe 'the
conceptual structure of the vocabulary at different periods, and then to
make comparisons between these cross-sections' (p 298) is fruitfully
developed by Coseriu in a number of illuminating instances — his analysis
of the alteration in the structure of the concept of 'old' as between Classical
Latin and Spanish (p 151) and that of family relationships (p 159) are
especially enlightening. For the investigation of this type of change the solid
foundation provided by the well-researched areas of Classical Latin or the
Romance languages in their modern form is essential. However, once the
investigation moves to a less well-documented period of language serious
difficulties arise, no less serious for not always being clearly recognized. For
example, Coseriu accepts without demur as an established fact the
Wartburg/Ullmann explanation by homonymic clash of the semantic shift
caused by the loss of *femur* and the change of meaning of *coxa* from 'hip' to
'thigh'. According to this explanation, the modern French *cuisse* means

---

[4] See also F. R. Palmer, *Semantics* (CUP, 1976), pp 14–15: 'Unfortunately, because they have
no clear theory of semantics, scholars interested in historical semantics have indulged in
vague statements . . .'.

[5] It is sometimes difficult to understand how modern semanticists can go out of their way to
ignore their own linguistic experience as well as all available evidence. Professor Palmer, for
instance, contrasts *arm-chair* and *fauteuil* as follows: 'whereas the presence of arms is probably
an essential characteristic for *arm-chair*, this is not necessarily so for *fauteuil*' (*Semantics*, p 22).
Ordinary native speakers of English back up the *OED* in deleting the word 'probably' from
this statement, whilst native speakers of French support the *Robert, Larousse, Dictionnaire du
Français Contemporain*, etc, in defining *fauteuil* as 'chaise à bras'. The result is that the
postulated contrast between *arm-chair* and *fauteuil* is shown to be false, thus damaging the
argument it was dreamed up to support.

'thigh' because the Latin *femur* 'thigh' became virtually indistinguishable from the coarse word *fimus* 'dung' and thus unusable in polite society. This avoidance of *femur* is assumed to have triggered off the shift in meaning of *coxa* from 'hip' to 'thigh'. However, the lack of hard evidence in the form of actual texts to support this conjecture over the long period of time between the Classical Latin era and the emergence of Old French must at least leave the door open to other possible interpretations. Not until the new dictionaries of Medieval Latin now in course of preparation are complete can we hope to have the necessary textual evidence to make an informed decision about the validity or otherwise of this clash postulated between *femur* and *fimus*, but close familiarity with the ways of medieval languages might at least instil a measure of cautious doubt. Although Stephen Ullmann sees the explanation by homonymic clash in this instance as protecting the semanticist 'against the pitfalls of a narrow associationism' (p 294), according to which *coxa* 'hip' would have been loosely used for the contiguous 'thigh', the historical semanticist, with his notorious lexeme-fixation, would have to point out that, however much we moderns might deplore the practice, the medieval world did not always distinguish between parts of the body with the same commendable rigour as the modern anatomist and was quite capable of using terms somewhat imprecisely, as the associationist theory would maintain. Not only is there the case of *bucca*, whose meaning changed from 'cheek' to 'mouth', that of *gueule*, meaning 'mouth' as well as 'throat' in medieval French,[6] and *furcele*, which Tobler-Lommatzsch gloss as: *Schlüsselbein; Gurgelbein; Herzgrube, Brust; Magengrube, Magen* (III, 2069), with abundant Old French quotations in support of all these renderings: in the case of *coxa* > *cuisse* itself, the starting-point for this enquiry, an Old Provençal translation renders the Latin *crura* 'legs' by *cueyssas*,[7] whilst a thirteenth-century northern French version of the Gospels describing the breaking of the legs of the crucified Christ uses *cuisses* for the Vulgate *crura* no less than three times.[8] In the light of concrete evidence of this kind it is difficult to accept the homonymic clash theory unless its proponents can advance a solid body of factual evidence which has so far not been forthcoming.

---

[6] See Tobler-Lommatzsch IV, 420–21.
[7] *La Vida del Glorios Sant Frances*, ed I. Arthur (Uppsala: Almqvist & Wiksell, 1955), p 230.
[8] Ed C. R. Sneddon, Oxford DPhil thesis, 1979, p 363.

The pitfalls lying in wait for the modern semanticist who would transplant into the medieval period his views on language acquired from study of the modern period and would attempt to apply them without reference even to the evidence readily available in the standard dictionaries are so great that the very idea of a structuralist approach to diachronic semantics might be unjustly called into question.

Dealing with the loss of the Latin pair *equus/equa* in French and their ultimate replacement by *cheval/jument* (pp 170ff), Coseriu sets up three historical phases of development: in the first phase *cheval* replaces *equus*, whilst *equa* is continued etymologically by the form *ive*; in the second phase the borrowed *cavale* comes in to take the place of *ive*: in the third phase *cavale* is itself ousted by *jument*. These changes are interpreted in the following way: firstly, with the introduction of *cavale* in place of *ive* there is a *changement onomasiologique*, says Coseriu, the name given to the animal having been changed; in the case of the replacement of *cavale* by *jument*, however, he would add to the *changement onomasiologique* a *changement sémasiologique*, since 'jument signifiait auparavant "bête de somme"' (p 171). In other words, the structural parallelism of the Latin pair *equus/equa* is broken on the male side only once, but definitively, by the replacement of *equus* by *cheval*, whilst on the female side the etymological *ive* is succeeded by *cavale*, a change of nomenclature only, and then *cavale* gives way to *jument*, where a genuine change of meaning is involved, the sense of the term moving from 'beast of burden' to 'mare'.

Coseriu's choice of example is excellent, but his explanation of the sequence of events is, unfortunately, no more than half a story incorrectly told, with the result that the picture given of the evolution of this small corner of French vocabulary is grossly misleading. Without attempting any personal research at all on this question, let us simply record the development as it emerges from a reading of the standard dictionaries of medieval French. Firstly, they make it immediately apparent that *cavale* is totally out of place here. Completely unknown to Tobler-Lommatzsch, it figures only once in the Godefroy *Complément* (IX, 11) in a quotation from La Boetie. The *Französisches Etymologisches Wörterbuch* (II, i 2) picks up Godefroy's quotation and explains that *cavale* is not a native French term but is introduced into France *in the middle of the sixteenth century* on account of 'dem regen export von hochwertigen zuchtpferden aus Italien'. When it is remembered that La Boetie was not only writing well outside the usually accepted limits of the medieval period, but that he came from Bordeaux anyway, it is difficult to attach much credence to the claim that *cavale* was a genuine medieval replacement for *ive* in northern France. In fact, rather than *cavale* being ousted by *jument* in the Middle Ages, as Coseriu suggests, the *FEW* puts the boot squarely on the other foot: '. . . so im wallon. und im frpr. ist *jument in neuerer zeit* (italics mine) von *cavale* verdrängt worden' (V, 64). Discounting *cavale*, therefore, as being completely anachronistic and geographically aberrant, we are left with *ive* and *jument*. Yet, here again, Godefroy and Tobler-Lommatzsch show that, far from the one following the other chronologically, these two existed for a long time — centuries even — in juxtaposition. The vitality of *ive* well into the thirteenth century is abundantly attested by many quotations and by variant forms, so much so that only now, in the second half of the twentieth century, is it 'im ersterben' from French dialects (*FEW* III, 233). Tobler-Lommatzsch even gives a quotation from a late twelfth-century *Vie de seint Thomas* in which both *ive* and *jument* are used in the same sentence with the same meaning, referring to the same animal:

> Sa jument fist ovrir e ses piez enz geter:
> De freit murut en l'ive, ainc n'i pot eschalfer   (IV, 1497, 25–7)

In place of Coseriu's neat and tidy sketch, then, in which *ive* is succeeded rectilinearly by *cavale* and then by *jument*, the dictionaries of Old French suggest a much less clear-cut diagram for the standard language in which *cavale* would not figure at all and in which *ive* and *jument* would stand together for a long time in the sense of 'mare'. A further complication to spoil the neatness of the diachronic development arises from the fact that *jument* did not change its meaning overnight, as it were. The dictionaries prove by their numerous examples that Coseriu's statement: '[jument] qui signifiait *auparavant* (italics mine) "bête de somme"' is factually incorrect. For some long time *jument* could mean either 'mare' or 'beast of burden', only context enabling the reader to determine which sense it meant.[9] Indeed, as late as the middle of the thirteenth century, the vernacular version of the Gospels referred to earlier uses *jument* for 'ass', 'beast of burden' in the parable of the Good Samaritan: '[Uns Samariens] . . . le mist sor sa jument et le mena en sa meson . . .'.[10]

[9] See Tobler-Lommatzsch IV, 1865–7.
[10] Sneddon, *op cit,* p 221.

The purpose of this protracted examination of the development of the Latin pair *equus/equa* is not to pour cold water on the idea that structural oppositions exist, but rather to insist that all available evidence, especially for the difficult medieval period, be fully considered before conclusions are drawn. In this particular instance, mention might well have been made of what look like promising attempts, originating in dialect, to re-create in French the type of closely related pair that existed in Latin. The *FEW* has the interesting feminine forms *chevautte/chouautte* (II, i 8), which would make possible a pair on the lines *chevau/chevautte*, and also mentions a form *jumente* (V, 64) that would presumably make possible another pair — *jument/jumente*. This kind of abortive attempt to establish structural oppositions represents the working of a genuine linguistic consciousness and cannot be ignored.

Wishing to illustrate the processes involved in *modification, remplacement* and *changement sémantique*, Coseriu uses as example the ousting of *chef* by *tête*, stating that '"chef" a été éliminé par "tête" de toute une série de ses emplois anciens' (p 171). The validity of this statement when viewed over the whole long history of recorded French cannot be denied, but the explanations given to show the semantic structural opposition of the two terms in the medieval period are at variance with the documentary evidence provided by the standard authorities. The argument put forward is as follows: 'une zone sémantique unique ("chef") a été divisée en deux zones différentes qui s'opposent ("chef" et "tête")' (p 171). Further, 'le signifiant "tête" a passé du signifié "crâne" au signifié "tête"' (*ibid*). Once again, let the dictionaries tell the story as recorded in their examples. Tobler-Lommatzsch shows both these statements to be factually incorrect. The 'zone sémantique unique' of *chef* was never all of a piece in attested French, whatever status the Latin *caput* may have enjoyed. Certainly as early as the twelfth century *teste* was regularly used in the sense of 'head', quite on a par with *chef* and not in opposition to it. What is more, the dictionary has not one single example of *teste* meaning 'skull'. On the other hand, there are numerous examples of a form *test/tés* meaning 'skull', but this is a masculine noun quite distinct from the feminine *teste* and repeatedly used in opposition to it:

> Jusqu'au test l'espee n'areste,
> Un os li tranche de la teste,
> Mes ne l'atoche an la cervele   (Tobler-Lommatzsch X, 279, 36–8)

Li aciers qui est enbatus
Parmi la teste jusqu'al test   (*ibid*, 48–9)
la teste et le test en deus moitiés li fent   (*ibid*, X, 280, 13–14)
(see also 16–17, 23–4, 48–9)

The real semantic picture, then, is once again more complicated, less neat and tidy than we are led to believe. Both *chef* and *teste* mean 'head', but both have other senses which sometimes coincide, but often do not: for example, both can mean 'end', 'top', etc, whilst only *teste* can mean 'pot', 'potsherd' as well as 'head', and only *chef* can mean 'chief', 'principal'. Furthermore, *chef* enters into a whole range of expressions, both literal and figurative — *hom del chief, tenir en chief, faire chief de, mettre a chief, de chief en chief, a chief de pose*, etc. Many of these expressions are peculiar to *chef*, but occasionally may be found with *teste*, as, for example, when *hom del chief* and *serf de la teste* both mean 'subject liable to tax', so that Philippe Mousket is able to ring the changes on *chef* and *teste* as follows:

Et vous, sire Saint Denis, hui
Qui om de ma teste jou sui,
Gardés ma couronne et mon cief . . .   (Tobler-Lommatzsch X, 284, 3–5)

There is no evidence at all for the postulated change of meaning of *teste* from 'skull' to 'head', but there is a genuine *remplacement*, as Coseriu calls it, when the early *test* 'skull' is dropped in the fourteenth century in favour of *crâne*. Interestingly enough, the introduction of the learned *crâne* < *cranium* is attributed by the etymological dictionaries to the surgeon Mondeville, writing in 1314: he is also the most recent author cited by Tobler-Lommatzsch to use *test* in the sense of 'skull' (X, 280, 30–4).

A similar simplification of the true linguistic situation lies behind the interesting diagram provided by Coseriu to show the replacement of the single Latin term *puer* by two terms in the Romance languages. If we are prepared to jump directly from Classical Latin to modern French, it is quite possible to maintain that *puer* has been replaced in French by *enfant* and *garçon*, but this is to exclude the medieval period. Whilst in modern French *enfant* and *garçon* often, but by no means always, reflect a difference of age,[11] their opposition in medieval French was quite different. Again, we

[11] Eg in addition to age, *garçon* can indicate (i) male sex as opposed to female: (of a baby) c'est un garçon ou une fille? (ii) subordinate position: garçon de salle, garçon de laboratoire (iii) condescension: un brave garçon (iv) unmarried status: rester garçon. *Enfant* has nothing to do with age in the following: l'enfant terrible d'un parti; Bien que plus d'un soit chenu, je vous dis que ce sont des enfants de chœur; je ne suis, hélas!, qu'un vieil enfant (all per *Petit Robert*).

L

need look no further than Tobler-Lommatzsch to find ample proof that *enfant* in Old French often means 'young man of high birth', without any apparent upper limit of age; *garçon* on the other hand, is very frequently used to indicate low or servile status, being also used as an insulting epithet, again without any age limit.[12] The structural opposition is therefore created in Old French, being absent from Latin — as Coseriu correctly states — but it is made on social grounds, the opposition of age being a creation of modern French.[13]

Professor Posner also, in her dislike of the historical semanticist's preoccupation with lexemes, advances arguments which are not supported by evidence, even from standard authorities. In her article on 'Homonymy, Polysemy and Semantic Change' referred to above, she postulates a new origin for *toilette*: 'Dare one suggest that the introduction of *toilette* represents a crossing of *serviette* and *touaille* . . .?' (p 3). The essential pre-condition for the acceptability of this suggestion is one of dating: *serviette* and *touaille* must have been attested in medieval French earlier than *toilette*. Yet, here again, the authoritative dictionaries appear to have simply been ignored and no other evidence is given which would lead to a revision of the datings they provide. According to Godefroy (VII, 732a), forms of *toilette* are found from 1287 onwards, whilst the earliest date given in the FEW for *serviette* (XI, 540b) is 1328. Unless these datings are to be set aside by the results of further research, the postulated crossing must be ruled out. Furthermore, consultation of the dictionaries would have enabled the writer to avoid serious misunderstanding of the development of the whole semantic field. She writes: 'The finer *toilette* was introduced into a lexical field that was already well-populated: *serviette* and *touaille*, *nappe* and *tablier* were . . . used for covering tables, . . .' (p 3). *Serviette*, however, could hardly be part of that lexical field if it did not come into French until some forty years after *toilette*. Nor can the rest of the statement withstand

---

[12] See Tobler-Lommatzsch III, 319–21 and IV, 111ff; also Phyllis Johnson, '*Huon de Bordeaux* et la sémantique de l'*enfes*', ZRPh 91 (1975), pp 69–78: 'Le héros a déjà vingt-deux ans: il ne saurait donc être question ici d'enfance au sens moderne d'âge biologique' (p 69).

[13] Even in the case of *puer* it looks as though the medieval period is capable of complicating the issue. Writing of the Children's Crusade of 1212, Brigitte Cazelles makes this very pertinent observation, although with no idea of structural semantics in her head at all: 'Cette croisade d'enfants groupe des *pueri* et des *juvenes*, termes qui, loin de désigner un âge, évoquent en 1212 un état social, car *pueri* et *juvenes* signifient "vagabonds" et "déclassés"'. *La Faiblesse chez Gautier de Coinci* (Stanford French and Italian Studies 14), Anma Libri, 1978, p 21.

comparison with the evidence provided by the dictionaries. The mention of 'the finer *toilette* . . .', for instance, is simply at odds with the facts. Both Godefroy and von Wartburg show that *toilette* was often used from the fourteenth right up into the seventeenth century as a wrapping material.[14] It can scarcely be claimed that traders would use fine cloth to wrap their wares. Similarly, the assertion that 'the *torchon* and *napperon* (>English *apron*) were usually reserved for rougher uses' flies in the face of all that the competent authorities explicitly illustrate by abundant quotation from medieval texts. *Torchon* and *napperon* are poles apart in texture, the former being coarse, even to the point of being used as *Arschwisch* (T.-L. X, 410), whilst *napperon* is used to mean 'table-cloth'. Godefroy (V, 468c) gives an example of a *naperon* being stolen and sold for 'trois solz parisis', a high price to pay if the material really were coarse; another of his examples shows that a fine, not a coarse cloth must be involved: 'Au haut du naperon de blanc lin'. Finally on this point, if '*serviette* and *touaille, nappe* and *tablier* were . . . used for covering tables', then the standard dictionaries of Old French need to be rewritten. *Nappe* and *tablier* were undoubtedly so used (Godefroy X, 190c and VII, 618a respectively), but *serviette* is a 'Tellertuch' for Tobler-Lommatzsch (IX, 564) and for Godefroy (X, 669b) a 'linge dont on se sert pour s'essuyer', whilst *touaille* is seen in a quotation given by Tobler-Lommatzsch *(loc cit)* as being synonymous with *serviette* and even in Godefroy's many examples (VII, 731b–c) not one can be read as justifying the translation 'table-cloth'.[15] What is needed here in order to come to a satisfactory interpretation of this particular area of vocabulary is not conjecture but concrete textual evidence, dated and localized, evidence that starts from the standard dictionaries and then goes on to draw upon documents not covered by them. Without the despised preoccupation with lexemes and the patient gathering of evidence by the benighted historical semanticist any semantic theory will be as fragile and vulnerable as those examined above.

During the 1930s, Trier's field theory, based on a study of the terms for knowledge in medieval German, introduced into historical semantics the study of coherent sections of vocabulary in place of the atomistic preoccupation with individual words in isolation. This important step forward

---

[14] 'morceau de toile servant à envelopper' Godefroy X, p 748a; 'morceau de toile servant à envelopper des vêtements, des objets précieux; . . . morceau de toile dont les tailleurs, les cordonniers, les libraires, etc, enveloppent les marchandises pour les livrer' *FEW* XIII, p 160a.

[15] Only in Tobler-Lommatzsch X, 339 is there one single example of *toailles* being used as a variant for *napes* 'tablecloth'.

has been universally acclaimed and rightly so. Yet when Bechtoldt, following in the footsteps of Trier, turned his attention to the intellectual vocabulary of French in the twelfth century,[16] his work found little echo, either at the time or since. The reason for this neglect would appear to be that, whilst Trier was able to present his findings as clear-cut and readily assimilable, Bechtoldt's results were far less so. Unlike Trier, whose range of texts consulted was minimal, Bechtoldt examined all the texts he could find in twelfth-century French containing words relating to the intellect. Time and again he finds himself having to make admissions such as these: 'Das Ungenaue, Vage ist nun einmal ein Charakteristikum mittelalterlicher Begriffe' (p 77); 'die häufige Unmöglichkeit, sich etwa zu Über-setzungszwecken für eine der drei Arten (*sc* of meaning) zu entscheiden . . .' (p 160). Time and again his quotations show that a word like *vezié* only acquires a precise meaning through context and can be applied to the sly cunning of the fox or to the God-given shrewdness of St Thomas in equal measure.[17] Whether Trier's clear-cut findings in medieval German would stand up against a new investigation using many more texts may be left as an open question, but there is little doubt that the somewhat indecisive results that emerge from Bechtoldt's work afford scant comfort to anyone who would seek to apply to the vocabulary of medieval French the same structural criteria as to that of Classical Latin or modern French. The essence of structural semantics would appear to be that terms of basically similar sense contain certain elements of meaning that distinguish their use in language. For example, it has long been recognized that the Classical Latin *albus* and *candidus*, whilst both meaning 'white', were distinguished by the element of brightness attaching to *candidus* and being absent from *albus*, the general term (Coseriu, *op cit* p 169).[18] Once we move, however, from the ordered, intellectual world of Classical Latin into the more fragmented, loosely structured society using Old French, we find that this pattern has altered: *albe/aube* has ceased to be used adjectivally, whilst *candidus* has been lost, only an isolated example of its use being found in the

[16] *Romanische Forschungen* 49 (1935), pp 21–180.

[17] 'Gupiz est mult luirez E forment veziez' Ph de Thaun, *Cumpoz* v 1777; 'Thomas fut vedziez, e Deux mult l'avança En sens e en conseilz' Guernes de Pont-Sainte-Maxence, *Vie de saint Thomas* v 251.

[18] See also A. Kristol, *Color: Les Langues romanes devant le phénomène de la Couleur* (Berne, 1978).

hybrid *Girart de Roussillon*. Otherwise, both *albus* and *candidus* have been replaced by the all-purpose Germanic borrowing *blanc*. From this and the previous examples given above, it would appear that, whatever structure the vocabulary of Old French may have had, it was not ordered on the lines of either Classical Latin or modern French.

The difficulty of semantic studies has often been said to stem from the fact that words seem to change their meanings in a quite haphazard way, to appear and disappear for reasons that sometimes escape us. This is particularly true in historical semantics, where a gap of many centuries has to be bridged. If any real progress is to be made along the road Stephen Ullmann glimpsed a generation ago, it can only be on the basis of a thorough understanding of the medieval civilization that used the language under examination. In other words, semantic theory must arise out of a mastery of the facts and not be imposed in ignorance or defiance of them.[19]

[19] I am grateful to Mr E. J. Hathaway for reading this article in draft and making some fruitful suggestions.

L*

Publications of Stephen Ullmann

Abbreviations: *ArchL* Archivum Linguisticum. *FM* Le Français Moderne. *FS* French Studies. *JPsych* Journal de Psychologie. *ML* Modern Languages. *MLR* Modern Language Review. *PMLA* Publications of the Modern Language Association of America. *RLR* Revue de Linguistique Romane. *YWMLS* The Year's Work in Modern Language Studies.

Books

Europe's Debt to the English Language: A Study of the influence of English on Dutch, German, French and Italian. London: Pilot Press, 1940. 154 pp.

The Epic of the Finnish Nation. London: Pilot Press, 1940. 128 pp.

Words and their Use. Man and Society Series. London: Muller and New York: Philosophical Library, 1951. 110 pp.
   Translations:
   Dawr al-Kalimah fī al-lughah. Transl by Muhamad Bishr. Cairo: Maktabat al-Shabāb, 1969. 240 pp.
   Go to sono yôhô, imiron nyûmon (Words and their Use; Introduction to semantics). Transl by Kitchitarô Sunuma and Atushi Hirato. Tokio: Bunka hyôron shuppan, 1973. 201 pp.

The Principles of Semantics. Glasgow University Publications 84. Glasgow: Jackson, 1951. xii + 314 pp. 2nd edn with additional chapter. Oxford: Blackwell and Glasgow: Jackson, 1957. Reprinted with additional bibliography 1959.
   Translations:
   Imi ron (Principles of semantics). Transl by Hideo Yamaguchi. Tokio: Kinokuniya, 1964. x + 370 pp. Reprinted 1966.
   Grundzüge der Semantik. Transl by Susanne Koopmann. Berlin: de Gruyter, 1967. x + 347 pp. 2nd edn, 1972.
   Principî di Semantica. Transl by Maria Modena Mayer and Anna Maria Diviso Finoli. Introduction by Gian Paolo Caprettini. Piccola Biblioteca Einaudi 317. Turin: Giulio Einaudi, 1977. xv + 447 pp.

Précis de Sémantique Française. Biblioteca Romanica series prima 9. Berne: Francke, 1952. 334 pp. 2nd edn, 1959. 3rd edn, 1965. 4th edn, 1969. 5th edn, 1975.

    Translation:

        Introducción a la semántica francesa. Transl and annotation by E. de Bustos Tovar. Publicaciones de la *Rivista de Filología Española* 15. Madrid: Inst Miguel de Cervantes, 1965. xvi + 448 pp. 2nd edn, 1974.

Style in the French Novel. London: Cambridge University Press, 1957. vii + 273 pp. Reprinted Oxford: Blackwell, 1964.

Imiron Kenkyū (Essays [Research] in Semantics). Transl by Hideo Yamaguchi. Tokio: Kenkyusha, 1958. vii + 95 pp. Reprint in translation of five articles dating from 1946 to 1956. 2nd edn, 1963. 3rd edn, 1971. 4th edn, 1977.

The Image in the Modern French Novel: Gide, Alain-Fournier, Proust, Camus. London: Cambridge University Press, 1960. viii + 315 pp. Reprinted Oxford: Blackwell, 1963.

Semantics: An Introduction to the Science of Meaning. Oxford: Blackwell, 1962. x + 278 pp. Reprinted 1964, 1967, 1970, 1972, 1977, 1981.

    Translations:

        Semántica: Introducción a la ciencia del significado. Transl by Juan Martín Ruiz-Werner. Biblioteca Cultura e Historia. Madrid: Aguilar, 1965. xv + 320 pp. 2nd edn, 1967. Reprinted 1970.

        La Semantica. Introduzione alla scienza del significato. Transl by Anna Baccarini and Luigi Rosiello; introduction by Luigi Rosiello. Coll di testi e studi: Linguistica e critica letteraria. Bologna: Il Mulino, 1966. x/iv + 434 pp. Reprinted 1970.

        Semântica. Transl by José Alberto Osório Mateus. Lisboa: Fundação Calouste Gulbenkian, 1967. 551 pp. 2nd edn, 1970.

        Grundzüge der Semantik. Die Bedeutung in sprachwissenschaftlicher Sicht. Transl by Susanne Koopmann. Frankfurt am Main: Fischer, 1967. xiv + 401 pp.

        Gengo to imi (Language and meaning). Transl by Yoshihiko Ikegami. Tokio: Taishûkan shoten, 1967. xvi + 382 pp.

Language and Style: Collected Papers. Language and Style series no 1. Oxford: Blackwell and New York: Barnes and Noble, 1964. ix + 270 pp.

Translations:

Lenguaje y estilo. Transl by Juan Martín Ruiz-Werner. Biblioteca Cultura e Historia. Madrid: Aguilar, 1968. xx + 322 pp.

Stile e linguaggio. Transl by Olga Rossi Devoto. La Cultura e il Tempo 20. Florence: Vallecchi, 1968. 339 pp.

Sprache und Stil. Aufsätze zur Semantik und Stylistik. Transl by Susanne Koopmann. Konzepte der Sprach- und Literaturwissenschaft 12. Tübingen: Niemeyer, 1972. 304 pp.

Meaning and Style: Collected Papers. Language and Style series no 14. Oxford: Blackwell, 1973. x + 175 pp.

Translation:

Significado y estilo. Transl by Juan García-Puente. Biblioteca Cultura e Historia. Madrid: Aguilar, 1979. xvi + 175 pp.

Work in Collaboration

Walther von Wartburg: *Einführung in Problematik und Methodik der Sprachwissenschaft*. Zweite, unter Mitwirkung von Stephan Ullmann verbesserte und erweiterte Auflage. Tübingen: Niemeyer, 1962. xiii + 248 pp. Translated into French by Pierre Maillard, 1963; into English by Joyce M. H. Reid, 1969; into Italian by Enrico Arcaini, 1971; into Portuguese by Maria Elisa Mascarenhas, 1975.

Articles

1936–45

'Olasz hatások a renaissance-kori angol irodalmi nyelvben' (Italian influences on the English literary language in the period of the Renaissance), *Studies in English Philology* No 1 (1936) (Publication of the Royal Hungarian Péter Pazmány University, English Institute), pp 50–88.

'Le passé défini et l'imparfait du subjonctif dans le théâtre contemporain', *FM* 6 (1938), pp 347–58.

'Hungarian Words in English', *Hungarian Quarterly* 4 (1939), pp 1–5.

'Morus Tamás Dialógusa a magyar-török háborúról' (Sir Thomas More's dialogue on the Turco-Hungarian Wars), *Archivum Philologicum* (Egyetemes Philologiai Közlöny) 1940, pp 255–9.

'Note sur la chronologie des anglicismes en français classique et postclassique', *FM* 8 (1940), pp 345–9.

'An Eighteenth-Century Comedy on Anglomania in France; B.-J. Saurin: L'Anglomane, ou l'Orpheline Léguée', *ML* 22 No 1 (Oct 1940), pp 9–16.

'A Jelentésváltozások Törvényszerüsége' (The law of semantic change), *Hungarian Psychological Review* 14 (1941), pp 1–7.

'The Rhythm of English Infiltration into Classical French', *ML* 23 No 2 (Dec 1941), pp 55–8.

'Anglomaniacs in Hungary a Century Ago', *Hungarian Quarterly* 6 (1941), pp 36–7.

'Types and Patterns of English Influence on the Languages of Western Europe', *ML* 24 No 1 (Dec 1942), pp 4–13.

'Laws of Language and Laws of Nature', *MLR* 37 (1943), pp 328–38.

'Romanticism and Synaesthesia', *PMLA* 60 (1945), pp 811–27.

'Anglicism and Anglophobia in Continental Literature', *ML* 27 (1945), pp 8–16, 47–50.

1946

'Les transpositions sensorielles chez Leconte de Lisle', *FM* 14 (1946), pp 23–40.

'Language and Meaning', *Word* 2 (1946), pp 113–26.

1947

'*Dada* au figuré', *FM* 15 (1947), p 214.

'L'art de la transposition dans la poésie de Théophile Gautier', *FM* 15 (1947), pp 265–86.

'Anglicisms in French: Notes on their Chronology, Range and Reception', *PMLA* 62 (1947), pp 1153–77.

1948

'The Vitality of the Past Definite in Racine', *FS* 2 (1948), pp 35–53.

1949

'Word-Form and Word-Meaning', *ArchL* 1 (1949), pp 126–39.

'Les anglicismes dans la poésie de Musset', *FM* 17 (1949), pp 25–32.

'Sur quelques anglicismes de Vigny', *FM* 17 (1949), pp 95–101.

'A propos d'*autrui* sujet', *FM* 17 (1949), pp 225–6.

'Esquisse d'une terminologie de la sémantique', *Actes du VIe Congrès International des Linguistes*, Paris 1948, ed Michel Lejeune (Paris: Klincksieck, 1949), pp 368–75.

1950

'The Stylistic Role of Anglicisms in Vigny', *FS* 4 (1950), pp 1–15.

1951

'Phonologie et point de vue structural en linguistique', *Critique* 7 (1951), pp 979–94.

'Le mot "sémantique"', *FM* 19 (1951), pp 201–2.

'La transposition dans la poésie lyrique de Hugo, des Odes et Ballades aux Contemplations', *FM* 19 (1951), pp 277–95.

'Couleur locale anglaise et théâtre français', *Mélanges de linguistique offerts à Albert Dauzat* (Paris: D'Artrey, 1951), pp 339–50.

'French Language', I 1940–48; II 1949: *YWMLS* 11 (1951), pp 10–26.

'French Language', 1950: *YWMLS* 12 (1951), pp 1–17.

1952

'Les tâches de la sémantique descriptive en français', *Bulletin de la Société Linguistique de Paris* 136 (1952), pp 14–32.

'Valeurs stylistiques de l'inversion dans *L'Education sentimentale*', *FM* 20 (1952), pp 175–88.

'Inversion as a Stylistic Device in the Contemporary French Novel', *MLR* 47 (1952), pp 165–80.

'Quelques principes de sémantique générale', *Orbis* 1 (1952), pp 171–5.

'French Language', 1951: *YWMLS* 13 (1952), pp 7–27.

1953

'A propos de *stylistique*. La date du mot en allemand', *FM* 21 (1953), p 49.

'*Chantant*, adjectif verbal', *FM* 21 (1953), p 246.

'Psychologie et Stylistique', *JPsych* 46 (1953), pp 133–56.

'Descriptive Semantics and Linguistic Typology', *Word* 9 (1953), pp 225–40.

'French Language', 1952: *YWMLS* 14 (1953), pp 6–27.

1954

'Transposition of Sensations in Proust's Imagery', *FS* 8 (1954), pp 28–43.
'*Cambrioler*', *FM* 22 (1954), p 44.
'The Prism of Language', *The Listener*, Vol 52, No 1325 (22 July 1954),
   pp 131–2.

1955

'L'inversion du sujet dans la prose romantique', *FM* 23 (1955), pp 23–38.
'Note sur la syntaxe de Flaubert. L'emploi de l'article indéfini avec des
   substantifs abstraits', *FM* 23 (1955), pp 257–9.

1956

'The Concept of Meaning in Linguistics', *ArchL* 8 (1956), pp 12–20.
'Un néologisme de Stendhal: *élégantiser*', *FM* 24 (1956), p 168.
'On the Descriptive Method in Semantics', *Proceedings of the Seventh
   International Congress of Linguistics, London 1952* (London, 1956),
   pp 198–201.

1957

'Glanures gidiennes', *FM* 25 (1957), pp 196–205.
'Historical Semantics and the Structure of the Vocabulary', *Miscelánea
   Homenaje a André Martinet. Estructuralismo e Historia* (La Laguna, 1957),
   Vol I, pp 289–303.

1958

'Orientations nouvelles en sémantique', *JPsych* 51 (1958), pp 338–57.
'Semantics at the Cross-Roads', *Universities Quarterly* 12, No 3 (May 1958),
   pp 250–60.

1959

'Sémantique et étymologie', *Cahiers de l'Association Internationale des
   Etudes Françaises* 11 (1959), pp 323–35.
'Un problème de reconstruction stylistique', *Atti dell' VIII Congresso
   Internazionale di Studi Romanzi, Firenze 1956* (Florence: Sansoni, 1959),
   Vol II, part 1, pp 465–9.

1960

'Le Vocabulaire, moule et norme de la pensée', *Actes du Colloque sur les problèmes de la personne* (Royaumont, Sept-Oct 1960; organized by the Ecole Pratique des Hautes Etudes, VIe Section, Centre de Recherches de Psychologie Comparative), pp 251–63, followed by a discussion, pp 265–9.

'Le point de vue structural en sémantique historique', *Lexicologie et Lexicographie françaises et romanes: Orientations et exigences actuelles,* Colloques internationaux du Centre National de la Recherche Scientifique, Strasbourg, Nov 1957 (Paris: Edns du CNRS, 1960), pp 85–7, followed by a discussion, pp 87–9.

1961

'L'image littéraire. Quelques questions de méthode', *Actes du VIIIe Congrès de la Fédération Internationale des Langues et Littératures Modernes,* Bibl de la Fac de Philosophie et Lettres de l'Université de Liège fasc 161 (Paris, 1961), pp 41–60.

'Choix et expressivité', *Actes du IXe Congrès International de Linguistique et Philologie Romanes, Lisboa 1959* (= *Boletím de Filologia* 19, 1961), pp 217–26.

1963

'Semantic Universals'. Chapter 8 of *Universals of Language,* ed Joseph H. Greenberg (Cambridge, Mass: MIT Press, 1963), pp 172–207. 2nd edn (paperback) 1966, pp 217–62. Reproduced in *Novoe v linguistike,* Russian translation of *Universals of Language* by B. A. Uspenskij, Moscow, 1970.

'Valasztas es kifejezo ertek' (Choice and expressive value), reprint from *Learned Communications of the Teacher Training High School of Szeged* (Szeged, 1963), pp 159–66.

1964

'Style et expressivité', *Cahiers de l'Association Internationale des Etudes Françaises* 16 (1964), pp 97–108.

'Sémantique et stylistique', *Mélanges de linguistique romane et de philologie médiévale offerts à M. Maurice Delbouille,* ed J. Renson (Gembloux: Duculot, 1964), vol I, pp 635–52.

1965

'George Thomas Clapton' (with P. M. W[etherill]), *FS* 19 (1965), pp 221–2.

'Images of Time and Memory in *Jean Santeuil*', *Currents of Thought in French Literature. Essays in Memory of G. T. Clapton*, ed J. C. Ireson (Oxford: Blackwell, 1965), pp 210–26.

'New Attitudes to Style', *A Review of English Literature* (ed A. Norman Jeffares), 6, No 2 (April 1965), pp 22–31.

Review Article on Maurice Leroy: *Les Grands Courants de la linguistique moderne* (Brussels: Presses Univ de Bruxelles and Paris: PUF, 1963), *Forum for Modern Language Studies* 1 (1965), pp 78–83.

'Synchronie et diachronie en sémantique', *Actes du Xe Congrès International de Linguistique et Philologie Romanes*, Strasbourg 1962, publiés par G. Straka (Paris: Klincksieck, 1965), pp 55–69.

1967

'Les idées linguistiques de Proust dans *Jean Santeuil*', *RLR* 31 (1967), pp 134–46.

'Où en sont les études de sémantique historique?', *Actes du Xe Congrès de la Fédération Internationale des Langues et Littératures Modernes*, publiés par Paul Vernois (Paris: Klincksieck, 1967), pp 105–22.

Review article on A. J. Greimas: *Sémantique structurale*, 'Langue et Langage' series (Paris: Larousse, 1966), *Lingua* 18 (1967), pp 296–303.

1968

'L'esthétique de l'image dans "Contre Sainte-Beuve" de Marcel Proust', *Festschrift Walther von Wartburg zum 80. Geburtstag, 18. Mai 1968*, herausgegeben von Kurt Baldinger (Tübingen: Niemeyer, 1968), pp 267–78.

'Où en sont les études de sémantique historique': summary of 1967 article with this title, in *Probleme der Semantik*, herausgegeben von W. Theodor Elwert, *Zeitschrift für französische Sprache und Literatur*, Beiheft NF 1 (Wiesbaden: Steiner, 1968), pp 1–2.

1970

'Proust's ideas on language and style as reflected in his correspondence', in *The French Language. Studies presented to Lewis Charles Harmer*, ed T. G. S. Combe and P. Rickard (London: Harrap, 1970), pp 211–34.

1971

'Alfred Ewert, 1891–1969', *Publications of the British Academy* 55, 1969 (1971), pp 377–89.

'Semantics', in *Linguistics at Large*: lectures presented by the Institute of Contemporary Arts, 1969–70, ed Noel Minnis (London: Gollancz and New York: Viking Press, 1971), pp 75–87.

'Stylistics and Semantics', in *Literary Style: a Symposium*, ed Seymour Chatman; papers presented at the International Symposium on Literary Style held at Bellagio, Italy, August 1969 (London: OUP, 1971), pp 133–52.

'Two Approaches to Style', in *Patterns of Literary Style, Yearbook of Comparative Criticism* vol 3, ed Joseph Strelka (University Park and London: Pennsylvania State Univ Press, 1971), pp 217–25.

1972

'Semantics', Current Trends in Linguistics series, ed Thomas A. Sebeok; vol 9, *Linguistics in Western Europe* (The Hague: Mouton, 1972), pp 343–94.

'The Writer and his Tools: Proust's views on language and on style in his letters to some critics', in *History and Structure of French. Essays in honour of Professor T. B. W. Reid*, ed F. J. Barnett, A. D. Crow, C. A. Robson, W. Rothwell, S. Ullmann (Oxford: Blackwell, 1972), pp 223–38.

1973

'How the Vocabulary Grows' (Presidential Address to the Modern Language Association), *ML* 56 (1973), pp 1–8.

'Lexicology: its principles and methods'. Review article on Josette Rey-Debove: *Etude linguistique et sémiotique des dictionnaires français contemporains* (= *Approaches to Semiotics* 13) (The Hague — Paris: Mouton, 1971), *Semiotica* 8 (1973), pp 276–86.

'Natural and Conventional Signs', *The Times Literary Supplement* 12 Oct 1973, p 1241.

1974

Words and their Meanings. Australian National University Lectures 1974. Canberra: ANU Press, 1974, 23 pp.

'Words at Work', *Hemisphere* 18 no 11 (Nov 1974), pp 9–11.

1975

'A word to the wise', *Hemisphere* 19 no 12 (Dec 1975), pp 33–5.

'Das Wesen der Bildlichkeit', in *Romanistische Stilforschung* (Darmstadt: Wissenschaftliche Buchgesellschaft, 1975), pp 254–95. Reprint of chapter 9 of the German translation of *Language and Style*, 1964 (see above).

'Natural and Conventional Signs', in *The Tell-tale Sign. A survey of Semiotics*, edited by Thomas A. Sebeok (Lisse, Netherlands: Peter de Ridder Press, 1975), pp 103–10.

1976

'Simile and Metaphor', *Studies in Greek, Italic and Indo-European Linguistics* offered to Leonard R. Palmer on the occasion of his seventieth birthday, 5 June 1976, edited by Anna Morpurgo Davies and Wolfgang Meid (Innsbruck 1976), pp 425–31.

'Structural and Componential Approaches to Semantics', *Semiotica* 17 (1976), pp 181–90.

1978

'Neue Richtungen in der Semantik', in *Strukturelle Bedeutungslehre* (Darmstadt: Wissenschaftliche Buchgesellschaft, 1978), pp 15–39. Translation by Uwe Petersen of the article 'Orientations nouvelles en sémantique' (see above, 1958).

Reviews

Ullmann reviewed a large number of works on Romance and general linguistics, French language, semantics, stylistics, and lexicology. Periodicals in which his contributions appeared include: *Archivum Linguisticum, French Studies, Italian Studies, The Journal of English and Germanic Philology, The Journal of Linguistics, Language, Le Français Moderne, Lingua, Medium Aevum, Modern Languages, The Modern Language Review, Romance Philology, Romanische Forschungen, Studia Linguistica, Word*, and *The Times Literary* and *Educational Supplements*.

T.E.H.

List of Subscribers

Mrs R. Adamson, University of Dundee
Professor D. E. Ager, University of Aston
Mrs E. M. Aldridge, The Polytechnic, Portsmouth
Emeritus Professor Ian W. Alexander, 2 Menai Dale, Siliwen Road, Bangor, Gwynedd
Emeritus Professor L. J. Austin, Jesus College, Cambridge

Professor Ivan Barko, University of Sydney
Dr Annie Barnes, Honorary Fellow of St Anne's College, Oxford
Emeritus Professor H. T. Barnwell, 7 Brookside, Hereford
Professor James Barr, 6 Fitzherbert Close, Iffley, Oxford
Dr W. A. Bennett, King's College, University of London
Dr David M. Bickerton, University of Glasgow
Sir Basil Blackwell, Publisher, Oxford
Dr T. C. Bookless, The Polytechnic, Bristol
Dr C. W. G. Boswell, Goldsmith's College, University of London
Professor M. M. Bowie, Queen Mary College, University of London
Professor Christopher N. L. Brooke, Gonville and Caius College, Cambridge
Mr and Mrs Geoffrey Bullock, 9 The Braid, Chesham
Dr Richard F. M. Byrn, University of Leeds

The Revd Professor George B. Caird, The Queen's College, Oxford
Dr J. Cameron Wilson, Jesus College, Cambridge
Mr D. W. Carter, 8 North Road, Horsforth, Leeds
Dr D. J. Charley, OBE, 25 Shaw Lane, Headingley, Leeds
Dr Dorothy Coleman, New Hall, Cambridge
Mr J. W. Coutts, 2 The Rosary, Holmer Green, High Wycombe
Dr D. A. Coward, University of Leeds
Dr J. Cremona, Trinity Hall, Cambridge

Mr A. D. Crow, Emeritus Fellow of Oriel College, Oxford
Miss H. V. Cummings, 24 Church Road, Barnes, London SW13

Sir Frederick Dainton, FRS, Fieldside, Water Eaton Lane, Oxford
Mr J. C. A. Davey, Basil Blackwell Ltd, 108 Cowley Road, Oxford
Mr and Mrs D. A. Davidson, 9 Foxcroft Green, Beckett's Park, Leeds
Professor G. A. Davies, University of Leeds
Mr and Mrs J. R. Dawson, 22 Helmsley Drive, Far Headingley, Leeds
Professor Wolf Dietrich, University of Münster, West Germany
Emeritus Professor A. H. Diverres, 23 Whiteshill Drive, Langland,
    Swansea

Emeritus Professor R. W. V. Elliott, Australian National University,
    Canberra
Professor H. L. Elvin, 4 Bulstrode Gardens, Cambridge
Emeritus Professor W. Theodor Elwert, University of Mainz, West
    Germany
Professor D. Ellis Evans, Jesus College, Oxford
Mr D. H. Evans, The Watermill, Galphay, Nr Ripon
Dr Howard Evans, The University, and Mrs Michelle Pépratx-Evans,
    Trinity and All Saints' College, Leeds
Dr and Mrs R. J. W. Evans, 83 Norreys Road, Cumnor, Oxford

Professor Alison Fairlie, 11 Parker Street, Cambridge
Professor Rudolf Filipović, University of Zagreb, Yugoslavia
Dr D. J. Firth, Newman College of Education, Birmingham
Dr Isabel Forbes, The Queen's University, Belfast
Dr Peter and Mrs Eva Friedlander, 18 Hunting Ridge Road, Greenwich,
    Conn, USA
Professor W. M. Frohock, Harvard University
Dr Cyril and Mrs A. M. Furst

Professor F. W. A. George, St David's University College, Lampeter
Professor Paul L. Ginestier, University of Hull
Mr M. J. Glencross, College of Ripon & York St John, Ripon
Mr Keith A. Goddard, The Queen's University, Belfast
Dr Keith Gore, Worcester College, Oxford
Dr Robert H. Griffiths, College of Ripon & York St John, Ripon

Emeritus Professor C. A. Hackett, Shawford Close, Shawford, Winchester
Mr Raymond Hargreaves, University of Leeds
Professor Martin B. Harris, University of Salford
Dr Roger Hawkins, University of Sheffield
Dr J. A. Hiddleston, Exeter College, Oxford
Dr J. H. Higginson, Oastfield, 12 St Lawrence Forstal, Canterbury
Professor Francis M. Higman, University of Nottingham
Professor Atsushi Hirata, Toyama University, Japan
Mr F. W. Hodcroft, St Cross College, Oxford
Mrs Ruth Holden, 21 Avondale Road, Ponteland, Newcastle upon Tyne
Mrs Anna Horvath, 40 Pleasant Bld, Toronto, Canada
Professor W. D. Howarth, University of Bristol

Professor Yoshihiko Ikegami, University of Tokyo, Japan
Professor J. C. Ireson, University of Hull
Dr B. S. J. Isserlin, 154 Otley Road, Leeds

Mrs Edna E. Jellinek, Apt 813, 199 Rollins Ave, Rockville, Maryland,
    USA
Mr F. W. Jessup, Wolfson College, Oxford
Dr Stanley Jones, University of Glasgow

Dr E. J. Kearns, University of Durham
Dr Elspeth Kennedy, St Hilda's College, Oxford
Emeritus Professor A. C. Keys, University of Auckland, NZ
Emeritus Professor R. C. Knight, 2 Greenfield Terrace, Sketty, Swansea
Valerie Komives, 2449 Mulberry, Bloomfield Hills, Michigan, USA
Professor F. B. J. Kuiper, University of Leiden, Holland

Professor Maija Lehtonen, University of Helsinki, Finland
Dr R. A. Lodge, University of Aberdeen
Emeritus Professor J. Lough, 1 St Hild's Lane, Durham
Mr Edwin A. Lovatt, University of Leeds
Dr Nigel Love, University of Cape Town
Emeritus Professor W. H. Lyons, University of Sheffield

Professor I. D. McFarlane, Wadham College, Oxford
Emeritus Professor J. C. Mahoney, University of Queensland, Australia

Professor Maria Manoliu, University of California at Davis, California, USA
Dr Charles P. Marie, 78 Chemin de la Montagne, Geneva
Dr Elisabeth Maxwell, Headington Hill Hall, Oxford
Mr Cedric R. P. May, University of Birmingham
Mrs S. A. Mearns, Royal Holloway College, University of London
Dr M. R. Morgan, Girton College, Cambridge
Professor Anna Morpurgo Davies, Somerville College, Oxford
Mr P. D. Morris, 7 Holt Park Grange, Leeds
Dr Peter Mühlhäusler, Linacre College, Oxford
Dr L. R. Muir, University of Leeds

Professor Alfred H. Nissan, 6A Dickel Road, Scarsdale, NY, USA
Mr Arthur Nockels, The Spinneys, Enstone, Oxford
Mr S. F. Noreiko, University of Hull

Mr M. H. Offord, University of Nottingham

Dr David L. Parris, Trinity College, Dublin
Mr J. M. S. Pasley, Magdalen College, Oxford
Dr D. G. Pattison, Magdalen College, Oxford
Dr Ian Pickup, University of Birmingham
Professor Rebecca Posner, St Hugh's College, Oxford
Dr C. J. Pountain, Queens' College, Cambridge
Professor Glanville Price, University College of Wales, Aberystwyth
Mr R. D. F. Pring-Mill, St Catherine's College, Oxford
Miss Margaret E. Proudlock-Dunbar, Samuel House, 1 Main Street, Forest Hill, Oxford

Professor Randolph Quirk, Senate House, University of London

Dr A. W. Raitt, Magdalen College, Oxford
Mr G. O. Rees and Dr Ann Rees, 51 Weetwood Lane, Leeds
Professor P. Rickard, Emmanuel College, Cambridge
Professor R. H. Robins, School of Oriental Studies, University of London
Mr A. D. Rothwell, 41 Cemetery Road, Mossley, Ashton-under-Lyne
Professor W. Rothwell, University of Manchester
Emeritus Professor C. Dana Rouillard, University of Toronto

Emeritus Professor P. E. Russell, 23 Belsyre Court, Woodstock Road, Oxford

Miss E. M. Rutson, St Anne's College, Oxford

Mrs Linda R. Ryder, Lecturer in French, University of Salford

Mrs O. L. Sayce, Somerville College, Oxford

Professor D. P. Scales, Australian National University, Canberra

Emeritus Professor Francis Scarfe, CBE, 433 Banbury Road, Oxford

Dr Ruth Schubert, Roonstr 26, Hamburg 20, West Germany

Dr Leslie Seiffert, Hertford College, Oxford

Professor Robert Shackleton, All Souls College, Oxford

Mr J. P. Short, University of Sheffield

Dr Ann Shukman, Old School House, Somerton, Oxford

Dr Catherine Slater, Lady Margaret Hall, Oxford

Mr and Mrs A. Smalley, 10 Holt Park Way, Leeds

Dr Sybil de Souza, 3 Marine Parade, Seaford, East Sussex

Professor N. C. W. Spence, Bedford College, University of London

Emeritus Professor J. S. Spink, 48 Woodside Park Road, London N12

Emeritus Professor W. McC. Stewart, University of Bristol

Dr G. M. Sutherland, University of Glasgow

Professor Noriko Terazu, Toyama University, Japan

Mrs C. P. Thurlow, 73 Otley Old Road, Leeds

Dr Christopher Todd, University of Leeds

Alice Tsotsorou, 24 Church Road, Barnes, London SW13

Sir Ronald and Lady Tunbridge, 9 Ancaster Road, Leeds

Dr Derek J. Turton, University of Victoria, Victoria, BC, Canada

Professor Kenneth Varty, University of Glasgow

Mr George Wardell, 145 Kidmore Road, Caversham, Reading

Mr and Mrs J. Weedon, 13 Brassy St, Deakin, Australia

Mr Alexander Weinreb, 1 Wentworth Court, Wentworth Avenue, London N3

Dr P. M. Wetherill, University of Manchester

Professor John R. Wilkie, University of Aberdeen

Mrs Juliet B. Wilkinson, The Digby, Sherborne, Dorset

Emeritus Professor Brian Woledge, 28A Dobbins Lane, Wendover,
  Aylesbury
Mr J. L. Woodhead, University of Leeds
Dr J. R. Woodhouse, St Cross College, Oxford
Dr B. B. Woodman, The Polytechnic, Leeds
Mr Roger Wright, University of Liverpool

A greatly enhanced subscription was contributed by the Modern Language
Association in recognition of Professor Ullmann's work for the MLA
(President, 1973).

The Library, University College of Wales, Aberystwyth
The Library, University of Bath
The Library, The Queen's University of Belfast
The Library, University of Bergen
Institut für Romanische Philologie, F.U. Berlin
Romanisches Seminar der Universität Bonn
The Library, University of Bradford
The Library, University of Bristol
The Library, Brock University, Canada
The Library, Girton College, Cambridge
The Library, Trinity Hall, Cambridge
J. W. Jagger Library, University of Cape Town
The Library, University of Dundee
The Library, University of East Anglia
The Library, University of Edinburgh
The Library, University of Exeter
Seminar für Romanische Philologie der Universität Göttingen
The Library, Harvard College
Brynmor Jones Library, University of Hull
The Library, St David's University College, Lampeter
Brotherton Library, University of Leeds
Department of Linguistics and Phonetics, University of Leeds
School of Education, University of Leeds

The Library, University of Leicester
The Library, University of Liverpool
The Library, Goldsmiths' College, University of London
The Library, Queen Mary College, London
The Library, University College, London
The Library, University of Technology, Loughborough
The Library, University of Newcastle upon Tyne
The Library, Christ Church, Oxford
Department of External Studies, University of Oxford
The Library, Hertford College, Oxford
The Library, Keble College, Oxford
The Library, Lady Margaret Hall, Oxford
The Library, Maison Française, Oxford
The Library, Merton College, Oxford
Modern Languages Faculty Library, Oxford
The Library, Pembroke College, Oxford
The Library, Somerville College, Oxford
The Library, St Anne's College, Oxford
The Library, St Edmund Hall, Oxford
The Library, St Peter's College, Oxford
The Library, Taylor Institution, Oxford
The Library, Worcester College, Oxford
The Library, University of St Andrews
Centre de Philologie Romane, Université de Strasbourg II
The Library, University of Sussex
The Library, University College of Swansea
Bibliothèque Interuniversitaire, Toulouse
The Library, Ulster Polytechnic
The Library, University of Wollongong, Australia